Modern Jazz Classics

Full Color Edition

K Kelly McElroy

Modern Jazz Classics Full Color Edition Copyright © 2017 by K Kelly McElroy.

All rights reserved. Printed in the United States of America. No part of this book may be used or reproduced in any manner whatsoever without written permission except in the case of brief quotations embodied in critical articles or reviews.

This book is a work of non-fiction.

For information contact: info@uptownmediaventures.com
Book and Cover design by Team Uptown

http://uptownmediaventures.com

ISBN: 978-1-68121-094-0

First Edition: March 2018

10 9 8 7 6 5 4 3 2 1

Dedicated to everyone who understands, or on the journey to understanding, the spiritual relevance of America's classical music - Jazz

Page left blank intentionally

Table of Contents

Foreword	9
Introduction	13
3 (Three) Sounds	15
Abbey Lincoln	16
Andrew Hill	17
Art Blakey	19
Art Pepper	21
Art Tatum	22
Benny Golson	23
Ben Webster	24
Bill Evans	25
Billy Harper	26
Bob Berg	28
Bobby Hutcherson	29
Bobby Watson	32
Booker Ervin	33
Branford Marsalis	34
Bud Powell	35
Cannonball Adderley	36

Charles Lloyd	**37**
Charles Mingus	**38**
Charlie Parker	**39**
Chet Baker	**41**
Clifford Brown	**42**
Courtney Pine	**43**
Dave Brubeck	**45**
David S. Ware	**46**
Dexter Gordon	**47**
Dizzy Gillespie	**48**
Donald Byrd	**49**
Duke Pearson	**51**
Elvin Jones	**52**
Fats Navarro	**53**
Frank Morgan	**54**
Freddie Hubbard	**55**
Gene Ammons	**58**
Gene Harris	**59**
Grachan Moncur III	**60**
Grant Green	**61**

Hank Mobley	**64**
Harold Land	**68**
Herbie Hancock	**69**
Herbie Mann	**71**
Horace Silver	**72**
Horace Tapscott	**74**
J.J. Johnson	**75**
Jackie McLean	**77**
Jazz Crusaders	**78**
Joe Henderson	**80**
Joe Sample	**83**
John Coltrane	**84**
John Klemmer	**88**
Julian Joseph	**89**
Kenny Garrett	**90**
Lee Morgan	**92**
McCoy Tyner	**97**
Miles Davis	**99**
Milt Jackson	**103**
Nancy Wilson	**105**

Nina Simone	**106**
Oliver Nelson	**107**
Ornette Coleman	**108**
Pharoah Sanders	**109**
Rahsaan Roland Kirk	**111**
Ramsey Lewis	**112**
Roy Hargrove	**113**
Sonny Rollins	**114**
Thad Jones	**115**
Thelonious Monk	**116**
Tina Brooks	**117**
Wayne Shorter	**118**
Wynton Kelly	**121**
Wynton Marsalis	**122**
Yusef Lateef	**123**
About the Author	**125**

Foreword

"The musician is the document. He is the information himself. The impact of stored information is transmitted not through records or archives, but through the human response to life."
-Ben Sidran,
Jazz Musicologist /Musician

That quote couldn't be more accurate if you needed a way to describe the era of Modern Jazz. While the era of Modern Jazz is generally said to have begun in the first years or so of the 1940s, its span is certainly a broad and variegated one. So why did the early 1940s come to arguably mark the cornerstone of the Modern Jazz era?

Sidran's Marshall Mcluhanesque trope references a post-modern reality we've probably all heard by now that "The Medium is The Message," from the title of his book by the same name. It was probably the perfect metaphoric overlay for what of was happening at the rise of Modern Jazz in 1940s, indeed, what was happening in the world at large. The world was virtually topsy-turvy; Hitler was on the loose, marauding the Western civilization strongholds of London, Poland, France - invading over 20 countries. Italy's Mussolini aka "Il Duce" *on* the Western end of Europe and Japan's Emperor Hirohito on the eastern extreme of the continent both joined Hitler. They "gangstered" the world unmercifully. That is, until Japan literally blew three of America's battleships out of the water at Pearl Harbor.

The popularity of bebop as a style of playing and its adoption as a kind of personal lifestyle for those who played it and their devotees was already mirroring strong indicators of the societal complexities of the time: Swing bands led by white bandleaders and, particularly, those few African-American leaders found it difficult to sustain bookings due the hard economics of the times. Records were banned from being manufactured due to the rubber shortage of the war, draft age musicians were siphoned off to become soldiers, midnight curfews (brown-outs), and probably the straw the broke the proverbial camel's back, African-American musicians watched the white swing bands prosper financially off of African-American jazz innovations for many years.

Birth of The Modern Jazz Era

This bebop, this birth of the Modern Jazz Era, if it was anything during this moment in world history, it certainly uncannily mirrored Sidran's insight that "...*The impact of stored information is transmitted not through records or archives, but through the human response to life.*" Bebop, to the untutored ear, sounded jittery, dissonant with unstructured melodies, unpredictable time signatures, speeded up, nervous, and, in a sense, cynical. In actuality what they were hearing was music that was purposeful and intent on mastering the higher skills to play complex chord progressions with rapid chord and key changes. Instrumental virtuosity and improvisation based on a combination of harmonic structures.

It could be said that these mostly young practitioners of this modern jazz expression knew something that the world would never be the same again; that all human kind was now living on an irrevocable edge of possible oblivion; that some rules of reality as they knew it were no longer valid. The dropping of the Atom bomb alone was the ultimate game changer. Finally, even as Jazz musicians, they had no choice but express what was on their minds and in their heart of hearts. Swing, for the most part, wasn't made for that. That was primarily for entertainment.

These were well-read young men, practically most of them were very race conscious. They affected accouterments of the intellectual like black horn-rimmed glasses, berets, pork pie hipster hats, Fezzes, reading up about Islam and Africa, taking Muslim names. In short, these were not their father's jazz fans who enjoyed swing. With the advent of bebop in this Modern Jazz era, the Jazz musician had little choice about who he needed to be if he was honest. He was an artist.

Members Only

It wasn't lost on African-American jazz musicians how their musical innovations and compositions were used by white band musicians from whom they never received credit or financial compensations. When jazz gigs dried up during the 40s, African-Americans accepted the reality that they were literally, as a whole, the "baddest cats" on the planet. This reality even manifested in referring to their instruments as an "axe," as in cutting down a jazz player who couldn't cut it on the bandstand. To sharpen their playing skills, bebop musicians purposely honed their musical understanding of complicated and tricky melodies, like Bird's "*Cherokee*," Benny Golson's "*Along Came Betty*," Monk's "*Ask Me Now*," and later Coltrane's "*Giant Steps*" to name a few.

Modern Jazz Classics

The modern jazz musicians were predominantly young at the outset, although there were more than a few of the old heads like Coleman Hawkins and Ben Webster from the swing era who had the skills to hang tough with the best of the young musical Turks. The wonderful manifestation of this rising Modern Jazz music is that its soil was incredibly rich so to speak, from which, by some accounts, over forty jazz sub-genres thrive until this present day beyond Hard Bop, Fusion, Acid Jazz, Funk Jazz, Soul Jazz, and many others.

The genius of this book is that the author K Kelly McElroy has made it not only manageable but quite enjoyable to have literally sifted through more than thousands of Modern Jazz albums and selected the recordings that represent the Quintessential best as jazz classics for this book with informative commentary to accompany each selection. This is a book you are sure to cherish for many years to come.

Art Nixon,
Master Poet
Los Angeles, California, March, 2017

Introduction

Modern Jazz Classics is intended to provide the reader an in-depth, yet not encyclopedic, purview into the musical life of significant contributors to the modern jazz era. There is some disagreement in certain circles, but generally the modern jazz era is deemed to have been invoked when the "bop" era started to bloom in the late 1940's.

The musical scene evolved in a dramatic way when the "bebop" players got away from the syncopation of the long-tenured "swing" era that lasted from the late 1910s through the late 1940s. With the epoch of the "bop" era, musicians were free to express their musical virtuosity without being "chained" onto a specific melody or rhythmic chord patterns.

Key early pioneers, of course, included Bud Powell, John "Dizzy" Gillespie, Kenny Clark, and the incomparable Charlie "Bird" Parker. "Bird" created the newly formed framework for the new music. The mass popularity of swing music did not follow with the advent of bop. However, the music called "jazz" was never more thrilling and exciting!

While the mass popularity of the swing era was dying, it still existed under the label "mainstream." Out of the bop branch of jazz grew a tributary of genres including: hard bop, modal, advant-garde, free, and various types of fusion expressions, which at that point strained to even necessarily qualify as "real" jazz.

Once the fusion era leaped into prominence in the 1970's, the modern jazz era waned, but it never has completely ceased to exist. Many great musicians from the 1980s and onward like David Murray, Wynton Marsalis, Billy Harper, Roy Hargrove, along with many others took a step back to modal and bop expressions – all, generally, with post-modern sensibilities.

Some "old-line" musicians like Dexter Gordon and Joe Henderson led a significant rebirth of modern jazz that lasted during through the 1990s. After, this rebirth of sorts, many club DJs started rediscovering classic jazz albums, especially from the modern jazz era, and utilized these classic sounds in combination with dance, house, electronic, hip-hop, and rap genres. Included in this book are many of the best recordings of the era.

Is jazz dead? Some may say so, yet I completely disagree. When a person discovers these true modern jazz gems, they are just as relevant now as they were half a century ago.

Jazz is America's classical music and continues to stand the test of time. While this book focuses on the modern jazz era, it would be remiss not to pay homage to all the wonderful musicians who paved the way for those musicians of the post-swing era including the father of American music Louis Armstrong, Count Basie, Bix Beiderbecke, Lester Young, Benny Goodman, Harry James, Chick Web, and the indefatigable William "Duke" Ellington.

Of course, the swing era greats had their precursors like Scott Joplin, James Europe, the New Orleans Rhythm Kings, "Jelly Roll" Morton, Sidney Bechet, "King" Oliver, "Bunk" Johnson, the mysterious Buddy Bolden, along with many others.

The hope is that the reader, whether a newbie or a jazz adherent, enjoys the simplicity of the layout of this book. Included is a selection rating system that rates the selection from Very Good $\mathcal{VG}$, Excellent $\mathcal{E}$, to Masterpiece $\mathcal{M}$. It is meant to inform and inspire all to spread the "gospel" of this most wonderful musical expression called "Jazz!"

K Kelly McElroy
Cleveland, Ohio
March 5, 2017

3 (Three) Sounds

Artist(s) Information

Gene Harris - Piano

Andrew Sumpkins - Double Bass

Bill Dowdy - Drums

Musical Background

The Three Sounds was a trio formed in 1956 that comprised of piano (Gene Harris), bass (Andrew Simpkins), and drums (Bill Dowdy). The trio released several albums, especially for the Blue Note label. Some of the key players that occasionally joined the Three Sounds were Lester Young, Stanley Turrentine, Sonny Stitt, Nat Adderley, and Lou Donaldson. The group disbanded in 1973, yet their small-group virtuosity has rarely been matched since then.

Some Key Albums and Musical Selections

Summertime *E*
Poinciana *VG*

Black Orchid *M*
Nature Boy *E*

Abbey Lincoln

Artist(s) Information

Anna Marie Wooldridge – Jazz Vocals

Musical Background

Abbey Lincoln was a dynamic jazz vocalist who wholeheartedly adopted the advent of the bop movement. Her vocal phrasing perfectly coalesced with the dynamics of bop, hard bop, modal, and even the avant-garde. Besides being a jazz vocalist, she was a songwriter, actress and civil rights activist. Her rendition of *Afro Blue* is incomparable.

Some Key Albums and Musical Selections

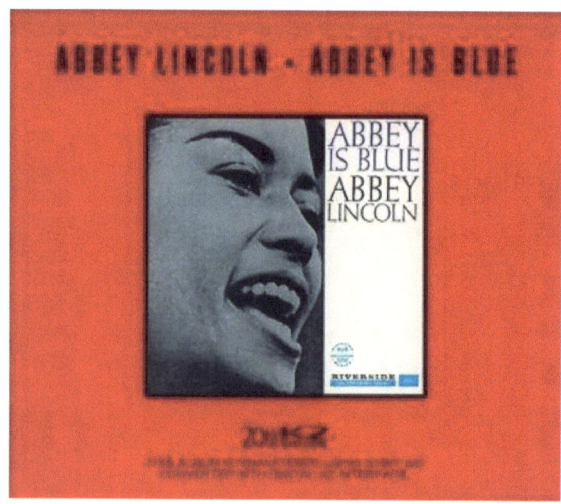

Afro Blue 𝓂
Let Up 𝓂

Nature Boy 𝓂

Modern Jazz Classics

Andrew Hill

Artist(s) Information

Andrew Hill – Piano, Celeste, harpsichord

Musical Background

With a style that "out avant-garded" even the most avant-garde players of his time, Andrew Hill was able to create compositions that created some of the most abstract, surreal, mood-altering yet coherent sounds. His most recognized work was a series of albums done for Blue Note records. Hill was a musician's musician and was not widely known beyond the jazz adherent scene. He was heavily involved in jazz education on a collegiate level. Hill perfectly displayed how to venture out musically, yet still remain firmly rooted in the jazz tradition.

Some Key Albums and Musical Selections

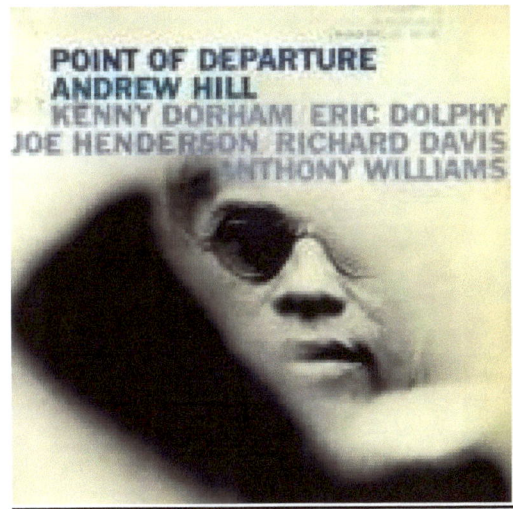

Flight 19 *VG*
Dedication *VG*

Smoke Stack *VG*
Verne *VG*
30 Pier Avenue *VG*

K Kelly McElroy

Pumpkin *E*
Cantarnos *M*

Subterfuge *E*
Tired Trade *E*

Siete Ocho *E*
Flea Flop *E*
Judgment *VG*
Reconciliation *VG*

Art Blakey

Artist(s) Information

Arthur Blakey aka Abdullah Ibn Buhaina – Drums, Band Leader

Musical Background

Art Blakey was the penultimate jazz pioneer as a band leader, with many of his talented sidemen establishing their own jazz groups. Some of the leaders that graduated from Art Blakey's "jazz university" were Freddie Hubbard, Lee Morgan, Benny Golson, Wayne Shorter, and Wynton Marsalis.

Blakey ushered in the "hard bop" movement of modern jazz with his thundering drum style that aptly complimented the fiery genre. Towards the end of his career he maintained that fire and thunder. His group, the Jazz Messengers, defined then and still define that soulful hard driving jazz.

Some Key Albums and Musical Selections

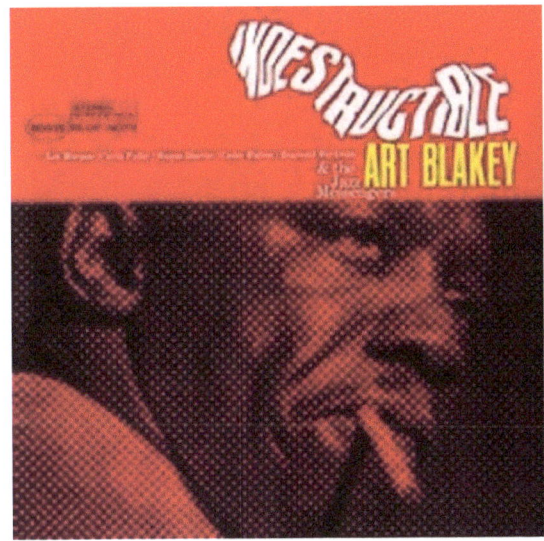 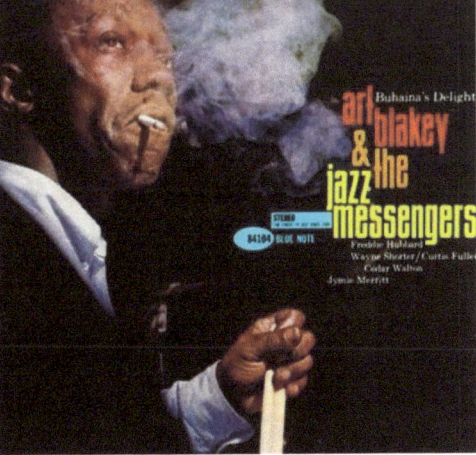

The Egyptian 𝓜 Backstage Sally 𝓔
Sortie 𝓔   Bu's Delight 𝓔
Mr. Jin 𝓔

Free for All 𝓂
The Core 𝓂

Hammer Head ℰ
Pensativa ℰ

Blue Lace 𝓂

Art Pepper

Artist(s) Information

Arthur Edward Pepper Jr. – Alto Saxophone

Musical Background

Sometimes a person can have all the talent in the world, yet tragedy remains always around the corner. Art Pepper was a trailblazer in the hugely popular, on college campuses, West Coast jazz - a lighter, much more airy counter to the fiery bebop genre. If his career was not interrupted by drug addiction and stints in prison his renown may have been even greater. Despite the bumps in the road, his musical achievements and accomplishments cannot be disputed.

Some Key Albums and Musical Selections

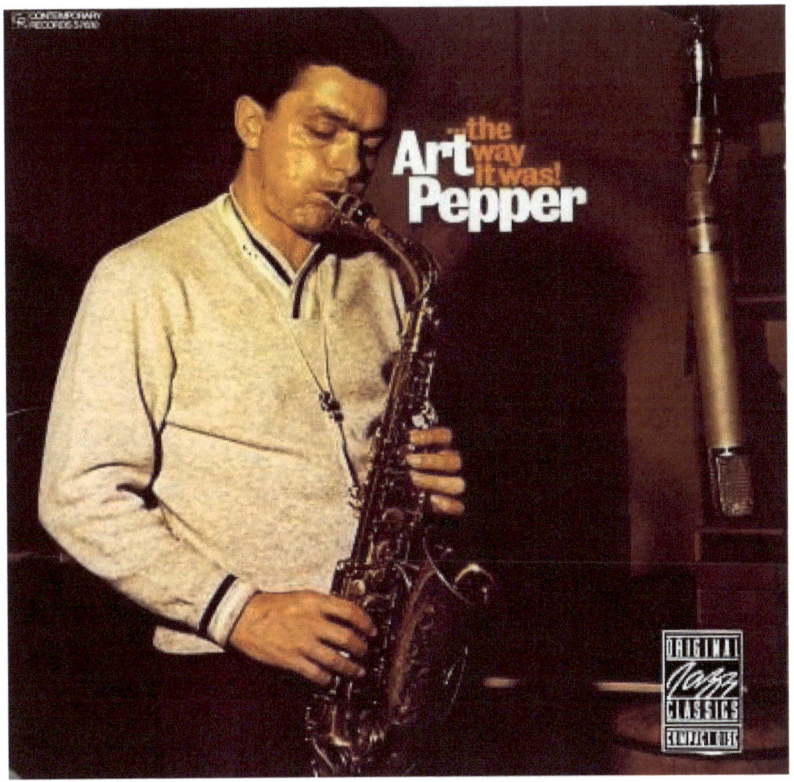

Autumn Leaves

Art Tatum

Artist(s) Information

Arthur Tatum Jr. - Piano

Musical Background

Art Tatum was a stride style pianist who was the ultimate virtuoso and is considered to be one of the greatest pianist of all time. Despite the fact that Tatum was nearly blind as a child he learned to play by ear, developing an uncanny ability to play accurately at double speed. Being a stride player, technically, Tatum is not likely to be considered part of the modern jazz era, but his influence on the art form is breathtakingly indisputable.

Some Key Albums and Musical Selections

A MUST have for piano enthusiasts.

Benny Golson

Artist(s) Information

Benny Golson – Tenor Saxophone

Musical Background

Benny Golson was immersed in the jazz scene early in his life and played with many later-to-be jazz greats such as Red Garland, Jimmy Heath, Philly Joe Jones, Red Rodney, Percy Heath, and the incomparable John Coltrane. Along the way he developed his chops playing bop and hard bop. Smartly, he diversified his musical endeavors by composing musical scores for many movies in Hollywood and teaching music on a collegiate level. His enterprising path clearly did not diminish his musical dexterity.

Some Key Albums and Musical Selections

Sock Cha

Ben Webster

Artist(s) Information

Benjamin Francis Webster - Saxophone

Musical Background

Ben Webster was on par with Coleman Hawkins and Lester Young during the heyday of the swing era. He blossomed during his stay with the Duke Ellington Orchestra during the 1930s and 40s. Despite being specifically know as a swing or mainstream player, Ben Webster could play with the best of the players in the modern jazz era including luminaries such as David Murray, Bennie Wallace, and Arche Shepp.

Some Key Albums and Musical Selections

Old Folks 𝄞
In a Mellow Tone 𝄞

Bill Evans

Artist(s) Information

William John Evans - Piano

Musical Background

Though seemingly underrated, Bill Evans was the consummate lyrical pianist who was "the" pianist on key tracks on Miles Davis' classic album *Kind of Blue*. After leaving Miles Davis' group in late 1959, Evans recorded some highly acclaimed albums as a bandleader. Many of his compositions have become standards.

Some Key Albums and Musical Selections

Gloria's Step (take 2) E
My Man's Gone Now VG

Gloria's Step (take 3) E
All of You (take 2) VG

Billy Harper

Artist(s) Information

Billy Harper - Tenor Saxophone

Musical Background

One of the jazzmen who carried the modern jazz era into the 1980s and beyond. Harper played with the jazz university itself, Art Blakey's Jazz Messengers, during the late 1960s. He later joined other luminaries such as Randy Weston and Thad Jones before going on to record a string of amazing albums during the 1970s.

Some Key Albums and Musical Selections

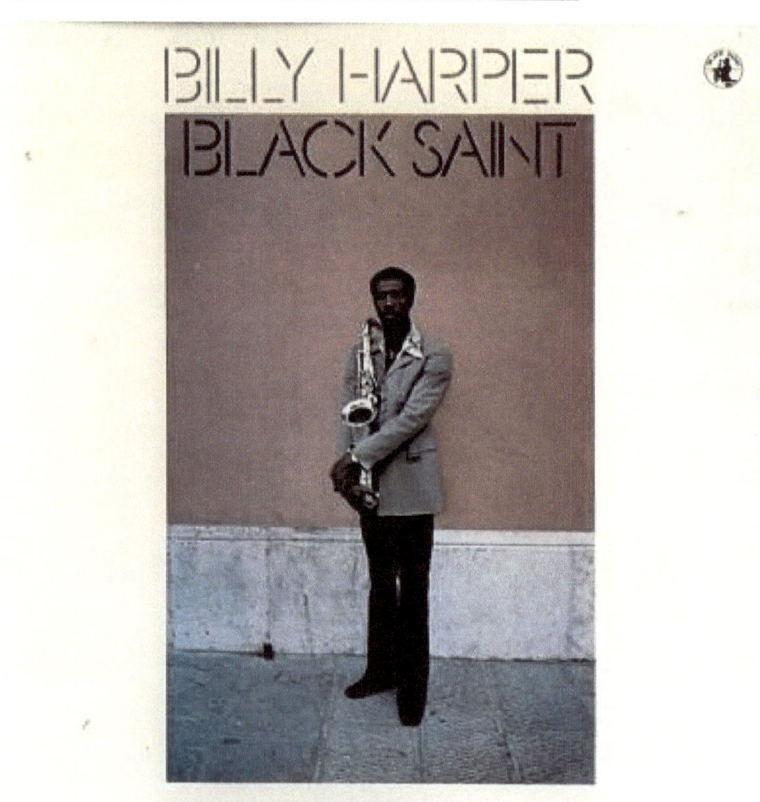

Call of the Wild and Peaceful Heart 𝓜
Croquet Ballet 𝓔   Dance Eternal Spirits, Dance! 𝓔

Modern Jazz Classics

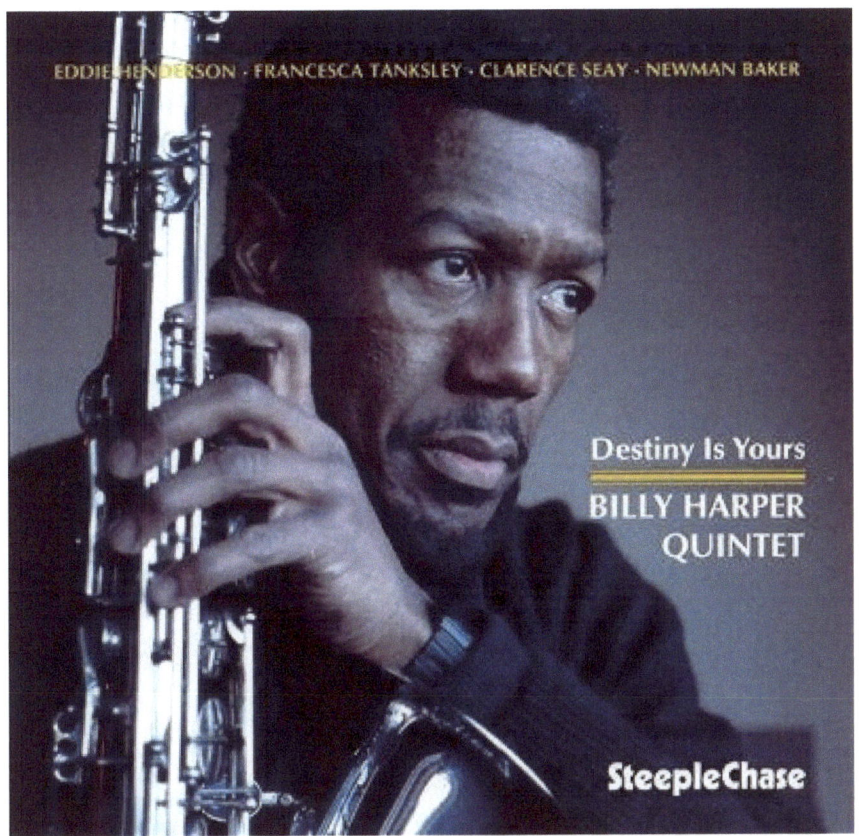

Destiny is Yours 𝓔
The One that Makes the Rain Stop 𝓔

Dance in the Question 𝓋𝑔
Groove from Heaven 𝓔

Illumination 𝓂
Priestess 𝓔
Calvary 𝓔

Bob Berg

Artist(s) Information

Robert Berg - Saxophone

Musical Background

Bob Berg, a graduate of the prestigious Julliard, played for a short time with Miles Davis' fusion band during the 1980s. He died too soon at age 51 but his musical legacy is well represented by the albums he released which show an affinity with the great players of jazz's past, all while displaying his own unique phrasing and musical sentiments.

Some Key Albums and Musical Selections

My Man's Gone Now E
No Trouble VG

Bobby Hutcherson

Artist(s) Information

Bobby Hutcherson – Vibraphone, Marimba

Musical Background

One of the few jazz luminaries who predominately played the vibraphone as a main instrument. He ranked with some of the other vibe greats like Milt Jackson. Hutcherson's discography spanned over 5 decades and many of his master works were recorded under the Blue Note label. His unique lyrical style was rarely matched.

Some Key Albums and Musical Selections

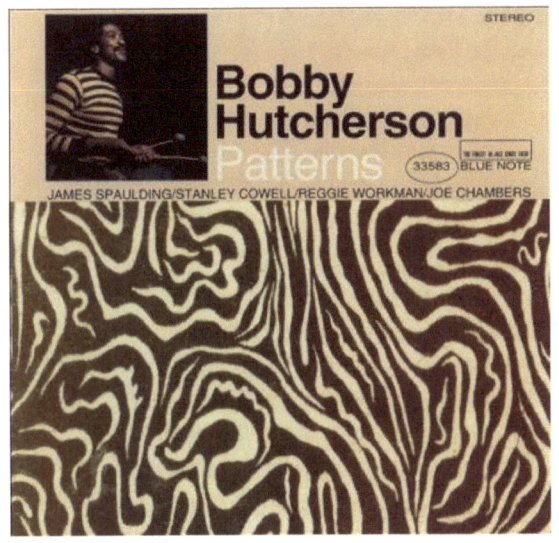
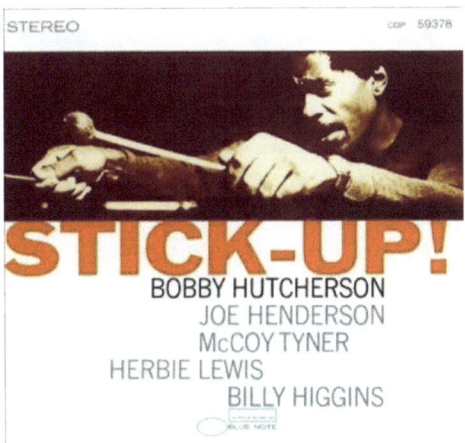

Effi *E*
Nocturnal *E*

8/4 Beat *E*
Summer Nights *VG*
Verse *M*

Mirrors *E*
For Duke P *VG*
Step Lightly *VG*
Bedouin *E*

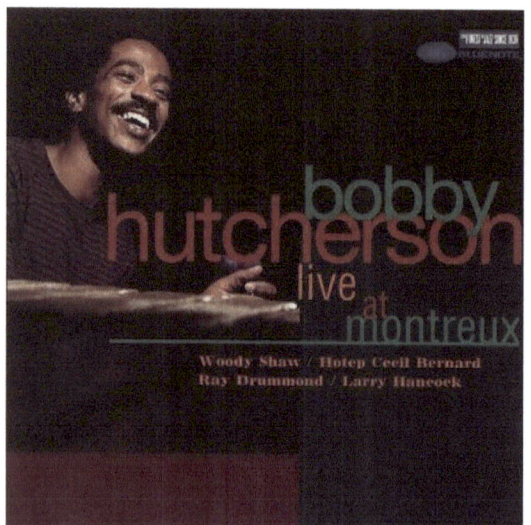

Anton's Bail *VG*
The Moontrane *E*
Farallone *E*

Modern Jazz Classics

Catta 𝓔   Les Noirs Marchant 𝓋𝑔

Aquarian Moon 𝓋𝑔
Maiden Voyage 𝓋𝑔
Head Start 𝓋𝑔

Bobby Watson

Artist(s) Information

Robert Michael Watson Jr. - Saxophone

Musical Background

Watson was involved with the inner circles of jazz, especially active in the New York jazz scene for many years. He is a composer and educator, along with his musical exploits. He has released many albums as a leader for various labels during the span of three decades. What makes Watson important is his scholarly pursuits as much as his vast musical repertoire.

Some Key Albums and Musical Selections

Appointment in Milano

Booker Ervin

Artist(s) Information

Booker Ervin – Tenor Saxophone

Musical Background

Booker Ervin was a consummate soul jazz player with a unique ability to create original phrasing that never sounded banal or trite. He died much too young at 39 years of age. Otherwise it would be assured that his notoriety would certainly be greater. Nevertheless, his body of work stands the test of time.

Some Key Albums and Musical Selections

Lunar Tune 𝓂
A Day to Mourn ℰ

Stolen Moments ℰ
Franess ℰ

Branford Marsalis

Artist(s) Information

Branford Marsalis – Tenor, Soprano, Baritone, and Alto Saxophone

Musical Background

Branford is one year senior than his famed younger brother Wynton Marsalis and is often overshadowed by his younger brother's puritanical fame as a "straight ahead" jazzman. Yes, Branford has "strayed' much further away from the original jazz gospels or doctrines than his brother, especially with his group Buckshot Lefonque, his stint as musical director for the *Tonight Show*, along with many other exploits. However, a closer look at Branford's body of work reveals the soul of a musical wanderer with a clear understanding of whence he came.

Some Key Albums and Musical Selections

The entire set is a complete Gas! 𝓶

Bud Powell

Artist(s) Information

Earl Rudolph Powell - Piano

Musical Background

Bud Powell was one of the most important figures in the formation of the newly created bebop school of jazz. Of course, like most of the early adherents, Powell sharpened his chops on the earlier swing music of the time. Powell showed as much promise as anyone of the other luminaries who ushered in the bop era. However, Powell's battles with mental illness and alcoholism would prevent him from living past the age of 41. Despite that fact, Powell left us with some of the most thrilling early bop piano, which is every bit as relevant today as it was back then.

Some Key Albums and Musical Selections

A MUST have for piano enthusiasts.

Cannonball Adderley

Artist(s) Information

Julian Edwin Adderley - Alto and Soprano Saxophone

Musical Background

A major presence during the "hard bop" era of the 1950s and 60s. Adderley masterfully linked the past with the modern jazz era and played with some of the greats of the time including Charles Lloyd, Yusef Lateef, Bobby Timmons, Bill Evans, along with the great Miles Davis and John Coltrane. Many of his tracks were later sampled in jazz influenced hip hop tracks by groups such as A Tribe Called Quest and Pharcyde.

Some Key Albums and Musical Selections

Autumn Leaves E   Love for Sale VG

Charles Lloyd

Artist(s) Information

Charles Lloyd - Tenor Saxophone

Musical Background

One of the most lyrical and melodic of the great saxophone players during the modern jazz era. Lloyd's musical output is reflected in a multitude of albums released from the mid-1960s through the new millennium. His career reflects the dedication of a true jazzman. Lloyd has collaborated with many of the greats of the time including Charlie Haden, Eric Dolphy, Billy Higgins, and Ornette Coleman.

Some Key Albums and Musical Selections

Forest Flower: Sunrise *E*
Forest Flower: Sunset *M*

K Kelly McElroy

Charles Mingus

Artist(s) Information

Charles Mingus Jr. – Double Bass

Musical Background

A musical zealot whose presence was often as dramatic as his compositions. A product of the turbulent 1950s and 60s, Mingus was greatly influenced by the bop movement and even played gigs with Charlie Parker himself before his own rise in recognition on the jazz scene. Mingus was unapologetically radical in voicing his opinions, musically or otherwise, about the civil rights movements that sprang out of the 1950s and 60s. Mingus composed many original pieces and is rightly compared to "Duke" Ellington as it related to making compositions for a big band.

Some Key Albums and Musical Selections

Fables of Faubus 𝓔

Wednesday Night Prayer Meeting 𝓋𝓰
I'll Remember April 𝓋𝓰

Modern Jazz Classics

Charlie Parker

Artist(s) Information

Charles Parker Jr. – Alto and Tenor Saxophone

Musical Background

One of the most thrilling and tragic stories in the historic annals of jazz. Charlie Parker, like Louis Armstrong before him, dramatically revolutionized the jazz world by introducing a style of play that would eventually be called "bop" or "bebop." Parker found a way to get away from the typical melodic phrasing by drastically altering the underlying chords, yet playing in a way to make the alterations coherent.

The rest is "history" as they say and Parker's legend holds sway. Yet, it's still a story of what could have been with his life and musical genius cut way too short at the age of 34, caused by hard living and drug addiction.

Some Key Albums and Musical Selections

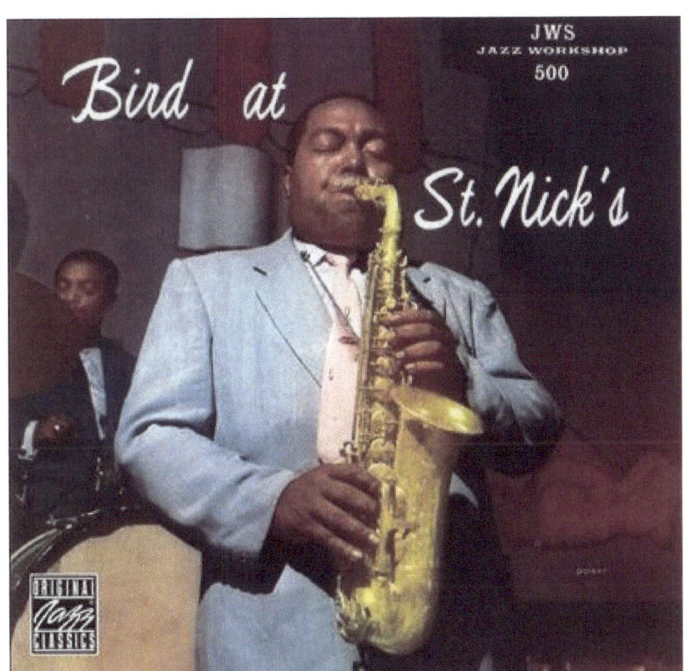

Confirmation 🎵

Not so great recording quality, but a must for Bop enthusiasts.

Again, not so perfect recording quality (but much better than *Bird at St. Nick's*).

Charlie Parker/Dizzy Gillespie – Bird & Diz

A very tight All-Star group and much better recording quality this go round.

Chet Baker

Artist(s) Information

Chesney Henry Baker – Trumpet, Flugelhorn, Jazz Vocals

Musical Background

Chet Baker was a major contributor to the West coast "cool jazz" movement during the 1950s and 60s. This genre, which was much more airy and ethereal than bop, became wildly popular on college campuses around the U.S. Eventually Baker became the face of the movement. Despite, battling drug addiction which began in the late 1950s, Baker continued to produce music until his untimely death at the age of 58.

Some Key Albums and Musical Selections

To Mickey's Memory

Clifford Brown

Artist(s) Information

Clifford "Brownie" Brown - Trumpet

Musical Background

One of the most dynamic trumpeters of the bebop era. Brown was a great paradox, however. He did not partake of drugs, nor was he inclined to drink alcohol – a dramatic departure from the vices that held sway on most of the great jazz musicians of the time. Brown played with many of the bop luminaries like Max Roach, Sonny Rollins, and Richie Powell.

What was sure to be a masterful and storied life in the jazz world was tragically cut short. Brown lost his life at the age of 25 when Richie Powell's wife accidently lost control of a vehicle she was driving with Powell and Brown as passengers. Despite such a fleeting presence, Brown's legacy is assured.

Some Key Albums and Musical Selections

Step Lightly *vg*
I'll Remember April *vg*
Flossie Lou *vg*

Courtney Pine

Artist(s) Information

Courtney Pine - Saxophone, Clarinet, Bass Clarinet, Flute, EWI, Keyboard

Musical Background

The modern jazz tradition has certainly continued beyond the borders of the United States – perhaps despite the growing indifference to the genre in the U.S. Courtney Pine, a product of London, England, carries on the tradition in masterful fashion at times. He sometimes mixed his reggae heritage with jazz and hip hop to devise wonderful blends – all the while holding true to the modern jazz tradition. To be able to pull off such a feat negates any argument of his musical genius.

Some Key Albums and Musical Selections

Sacrifice 𝄞   **Prismic Omnipotence** 𝄞

The Holy Grail Pts. 1 – 3

The Sepia Love Song
Una Muy Bonita
Up Behind the Beat
Time to Go Home
A Slaves Tale

Dave Brubeck

Artist(s) Information

David Warren Brubeck - Piano

Musical Background

Very few have left a musical legacy like Dave Brubeck. He was a pioneering force especially in the West coast cool jazz and third stream genres. Brubeck's musical career spanned seven decades and he was featured in 1954 on the cover of *Time* magazine, ahead of the maestro himself, Duke Ellington. Despite his legion of musical accomplishments, his claim to fame will always be his piece de resistance - the title composition of his most noted album *Take Five*.

Some Key Albums and Musical Selections

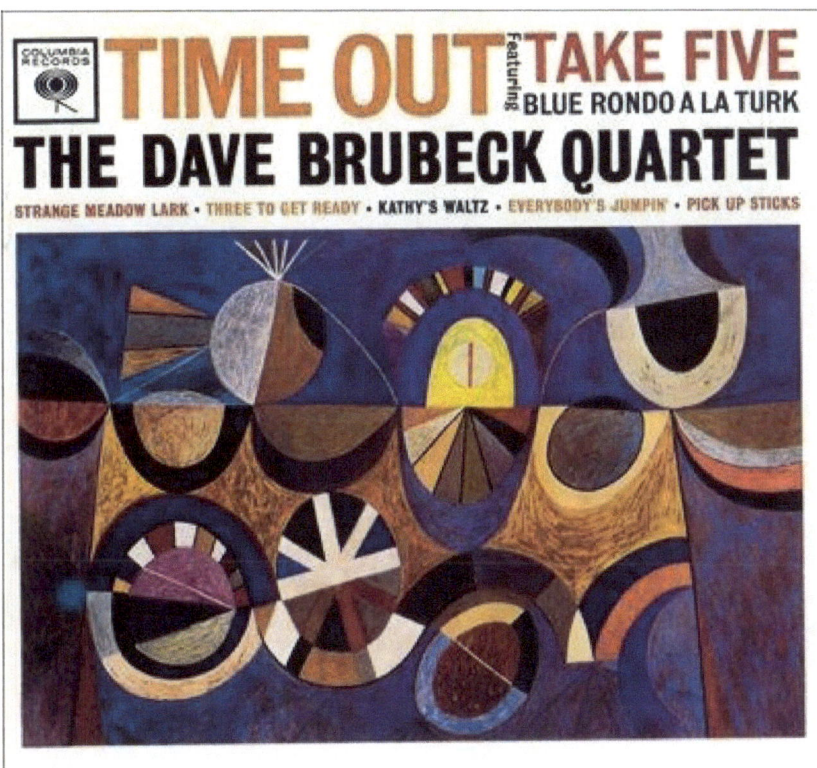

Blue Rondo a la Turk 𝓔   Take Five 𝓜

David S. Ware

Artist(s) Information

David Spencer Ware - Saxophone

Musical Background

Ware carried on the modern jazz tradition into late 1970s and beyond with a penchant for the avant-garde. Ware's discography became vast and extremely consistent as he toured across Europe and the U.S. Though not accessible to all jazz adherents, his album, *Flight of I*, remains one of his classic expressions.

Some Key Albums and Musical Selections

Aquarian Sound

Dexter Gordon

Artist(s) Information

Dexter Gordon – Tenor and Soprano Saxophone

Musical Background

Dexter Gordon personally witnessed much of the history and development of jazz, having played during the swing, bop, and hard bop eras. Despite relative success in the U.S., Gordon moved to Europe due to the social climate and overt racism of the times in the 1960s. He stayed active in his art and played with many noteworthy musicians such as Bud Powell, Ben Webster, Freddie Hubbard, Kenny Drew, and Bobby Hutcherson.

In 1976, Gordon finally returned to the U.S. for good and recorded a gig at the Village Vanguard in New York that ultimately became the signpost for the revival of bop and modern jazz – the album, *Homecoming*.

Some Key Albums and Musical Selections

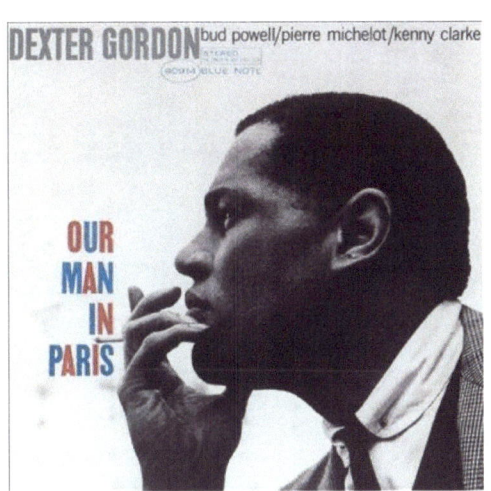

A Night in Tunisia

Tanya *M*
Coppin' the Haven *M*

Dizzy Gillespie

Artist(s) Information

John Burkes Gillespie - Trumpet, Piano, Jazz Vocals

Musical Background

One of the major figures in the development of the bop genre, along with Charlie Parker. Gillespie was the ultimate virtuoso who also infused his style and charm onto the scene with his horn-rimmed glasses, berets, and hipster jargon. He infused Afro-Cuban music into the genre and the rest would be bebop history in the making. Jazz would never be the same after Gillespie's exploits and his legacy as one of the progenitors of the bop genre is firmly cemented in the annals of time.

Some Key Albums and Musical Selections

Swing Low, Sweet Cadillac E
Mas Que Nada VG
Kush E

Modern Jazz Classics

Donald Byrd

Artist(s) Information

Donaldson Toussaint L'Ouverture Byrd II – Trumpet, Flugelhorn, Vocals

Musical Background

One of the great trumpeters who recorded on the famed *Blue Note* label. He shot out a string of hard bop and modal jazz hits during the 1960s. If his output ceased at that point he would be considered an important jazz trumpeter of the time. However, with the epoch of the 1970s, Byrd helped usher in the fusion era and helped bring throngs of otherwise neophytes to Blue Note, with his combination of jazz and soul, who probably would never have even came close to straight ahead jazz.

Some Key Albums and Musical Selections

   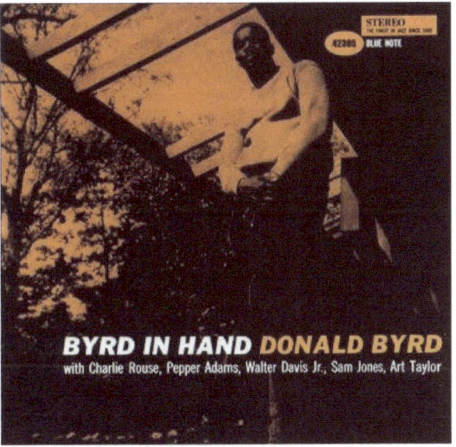

My Girl Shirl   **Here I Am**

French Spice 𝓔   Free Form 𝓜   Three Wishes 𝓔

Elijah 𝓥𝓖
The Black Disciple 𝓔
Beast of Burden 𝓥𝓖
Cristo Redentor 𝓜
Chant 𝓥𝓖

Duke Pearson

Artist(s) Information

Columbus Calvin Pearson, Jr - Piano

Musical Background

As far as composers and arrangers go, Duke Pearson was only a step behind such greats as Charles Mingus or maybe an extra step behind the great Duke Ellington. In any event, Duke Pearson left an indelible mark on the jazz lexicon with a string of albums that spanned from the 1950s until 1970s. Pearson played a pivotal role in producing many of the records under the Blue Note label ranging from big band to hard bop and everything in between. Albums under Pearson's leadership reflect his invaluable presence.

Some Key Albums and Musical Selections

Amanda *E*　　　　　　　Wahoo *M*
Farewell Machelle *VG*　　Bedouin *M*　　ESP (Extrasensory Perception) *VG*

Elvin Jones

Artist(s) Information

Elvin Ray Jones – Drums, Percussion

Musical Background

The drummer for John Coltrane's band from 1960 to 1966. Jones, though significantly recorded as a leader, rarely is noted as such. Jones will always be remember as one of the integral members of Coltrane's ensemble that took the jazz world by storm. Despite this fact, Jones led an influential music career after he departed from Coltrane's group. Yet, no matter how many albums he recorded or how many key musicians he played with, Jones' contribution to Coltrane's legacy cannot be understated.

Some Key Albums and Musical Selections

Ranchy Rita

Fats Navarro

Artist(s) Information

Theodore Navarro - Trumpet

Musical Background

Another tragic story. "Fats" Navarro was the quintessential bop trumpeter during the 1940s. His lyricism was unmatched and he even played with Charlie Parker for a time. He was in great demand but a heroin addiction, tuberculosis, and weight issues (his nickname was "Fat Girl") prematurely halted what was promising to be a stellar musical career.

Some Key Albums and Musical Selections

Historical Bop at its finest! 𝓂

Frank Morgan

Artist(s) Information

Frank Morgan – Alto Saxophone

Musical Background

Frank Morgan was exposed to many of the greats as he grew up, associated with, and even played with, or behind, the likes of Billie Holiday and Josephine Baker. In later years, in the 1950s, as a band leader, he played with Bobby Timmons and Jack Shelton. Unfortunately Morgan's progress was derailed by a drug addiction that led to intermitted prison sentences. Despite these setbacks Morgan became a leading figure in the post-bop revival in the 1980s.

Some Key Albums and Musical Selections

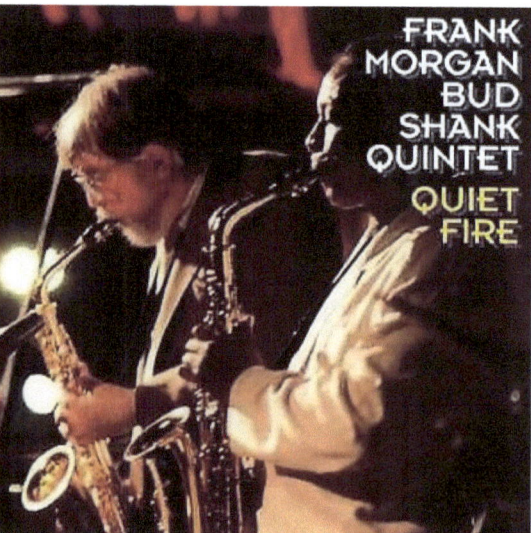

Footprints

Phantom's Progress
Quiet Fire

Freddie Hubbard

Artist(s) Information

Frederick Dewayne Hubbard -Trumpet, Flugelhorn, Cornet, French Horn, <u>Mellophone</u>

Musical Background

Freddie Hubbard was one of the most prolific recording artists on the Blue Note label. Hubbard was a notable sideman for Ornette Coleman, Art Blakey, and John Coltrane in the early 1960s. Eventually he ventured out to record as a leader and recorded many albums under various labels like Impulse!, Atlantic, Columbia, and CTI. His playing styled ranged from bop, hard bop, modal, and fusion. Taking the time to listen to Hubbard's musical works would prove to be a valuable history lesson for any jazz aficionado.

Some Key Albums and Musical Selections

Father and Son *VG*
Nostrand and Fulton *E*
Assunta *M*

Summertime $\mathcal{E}$ **The 7th Day** $\mathcal{M}$

Luana $\mathcal{E}$
Osie Mae $\mathcal{VG}$
Earmin Jr. $\mathcal{VG}$

Modern Jazz Classics

You're My Everything VG **Prophet Jennings** VG
Hub-Tones E

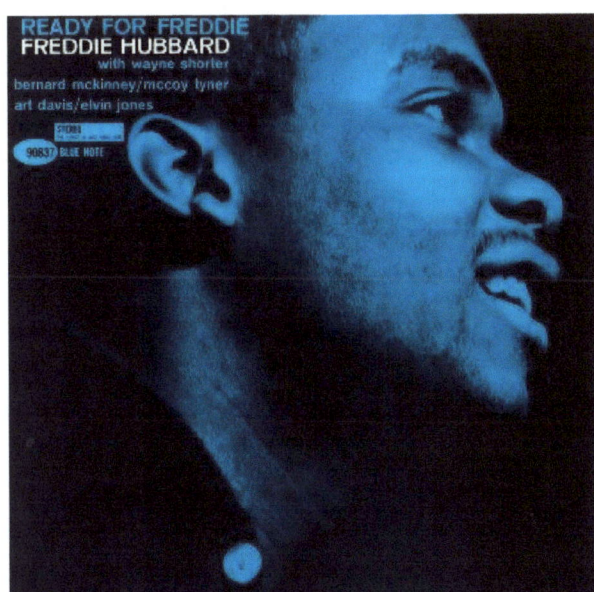

Arietis VG
Crisis M

Gene Ammons

Artist(s) Information

Eugene "Jug" Ammons – Tenor Saxophone

Musical Background

Gene Ammons continued the legacy of his father, pianists Albert Ammons. Ammons is recognized as a major contributor to the popular soul jazz genre of the mid-1960s. Ammon's compositions and playing style reflected his coalescing of R & B and the blues with jazz sentiments. Two prison stints for drug possession did not derail Ammon's powerful musical legacy.

Some Key Albums and Musical Selections

Jungle Strut *vg*   Feeling Good *m*   Blue Velvet *g*

Gene Harris

Artist(s) Information

Eugene Harris – Piano, Keyboards, Hammond B3

Musical Background

Gene Harris was the anchor of the Three Sounds which included bassist Andy Simpkins and drummer Bill Dowdy. Harris' musical exploits went beyond his connection with the Three Sounds, yet his musical legacy in soul jazz began and continues with the Three Sounds as reflected by the group's stellar recordings on Mercury, Blue Note, along with other record labels of the time.

Some Key Albums and Musical Selections

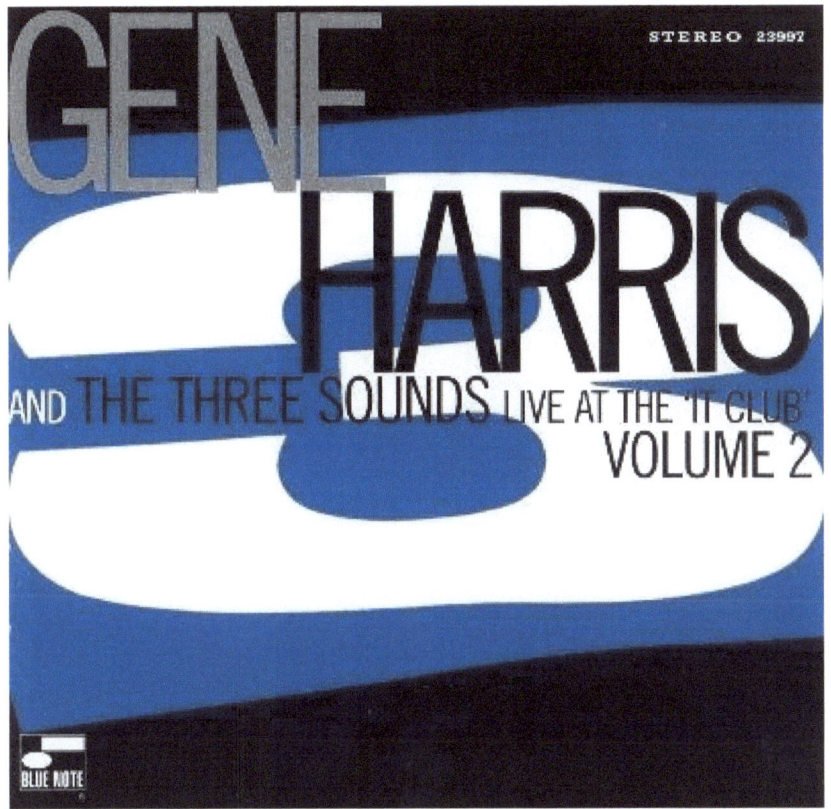

Black Fox *VG*   Apollo 21 *VG*
Eleanor Rigby *E*   Come Together *E*

Grachan Moncur III

Artist(s) Information

Grachan Moncur III - Trombone

Musical Background

One of the few stellar trombonists of the modern jazz era. Moncur played with Ray Charles' group in the late 1950s and early 60s after he graduated from high school. Eventually he played with such greats who recorded under the Blue Note label like Jackie McClean, Wayne Shorter, Herbie Hancock, and the incomparable Lee Morgan. Though not prolific in album discography, Moncur certainly left his mark on the modern jazz era.

Some Key Albums and Musical Selections

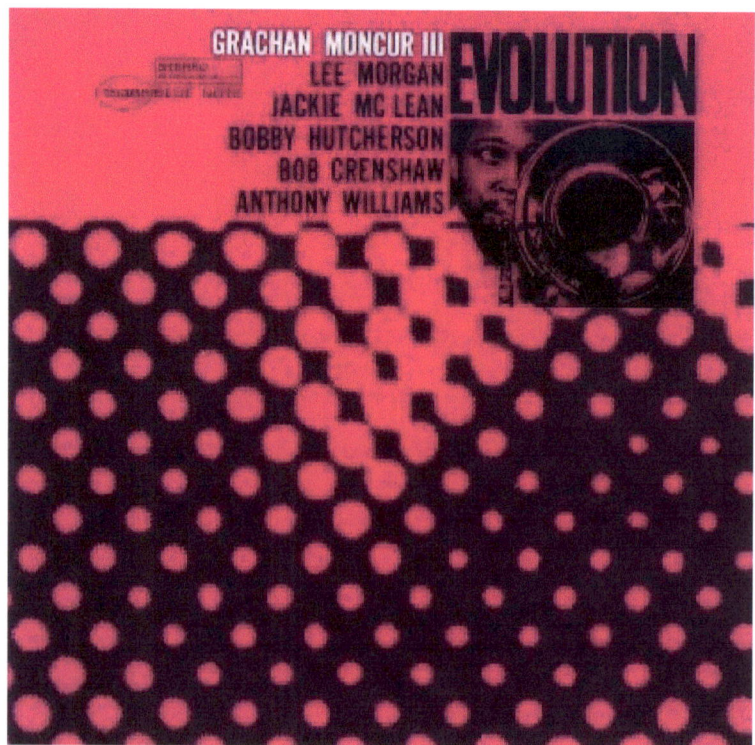

Grant Green

Artist(s) Information

Grant Green - Guitar

Musical Background

Grant Green was one of the few major guitarists to be associated with the Blue Note label. In fact, green was one of Blue Note's most prolific artists in the 1960s. Green played every style imaginable from the blues, soul jazz, post-bop, and modal. Green recorded so much that many of his albums were released posthumously. Tragically, Green died young at the age of 43 due to heart complications. Nevertheless, his star still shines brightly with his legacy of musical jewels.

Some Key Albums and Musical Selections

Time to Remember E
Sookie, Sookie VG

Hurt So Bad E

Joshua Fit the Battle of Jericho 🎵
Go Down Moses 🎵 Sometimes I Feel Like a Motherless Child 🎵

Idle Moments 🎵
Jean De Fleur 🎵

Modern Jazz Classics

Matador 𝓔
Green Jeans 𝓔

My Favorite Things 𝓔
Bedouin 𝓜

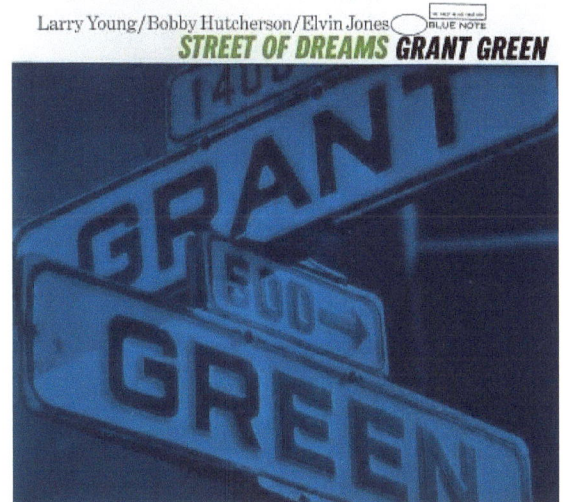

Lazy Afternoon 𝓔

Hank Mobley

Artist(s) Information

Henry Mobley – Tenor Saxophone

Musical Background

Hank Mobley was a beacon in the modern jazz age. Aptly described as the "middle weight champion," by producer Leonard feather because Mobley was not as aggressive as Coltrane, but was not as mellow as players like Stan Getz. Mobley is very well represented as a leader and sideman, mostly under the Blue Note label. Many think of Mobley as underrated compared to his contemporaries. His musical accomplishments don't belie this assertion.

Some Key Albums and Musical Selections

Lookin' East

Cute 'N Pretty

Modern Jazz Classics

This I Dig of You *vg*   Split Feelins' *vg*   If I Should Loose You *vg*

Chain Reaction *E*
Soft Impressions *vg*
The Feelins' Good *E*

A Dab of This and That *vg*
No Argument *vg*

Far Away Lands *E*
Bossa for Baby *E*

Carolyn *E*
No Room for Squares *E*

Modern Jazz Classics

The Morning After 𝓜 Venus Di Mildew 𝓔
Ace Deuce Trey 𝓋𝓰 3rd Time Around 𝓔

Dippin' 𝓋𝓰
The Vamp 𝓔

K Kelly McElroy

Harold Land

Artist(s) Information

Harold de Vance Land – Tenor Saxophone

Musical Background

Harold Land proved to be a laudable post-bop and hard bop saxophonist. His contribution to the modern jazz era was established not just as a player but as an educator on the collegiate level. Though not as acclaimed as some of the greats, Harold Land certainly left his mark.

Some Key Albums and Musical Selections

Little Chris

Herbie Hancock

Artist(s) Information

Herbert Jeffrey Hancock – Piano, Electric Piano, Synthesizers, Keyboards

Musical Background

Herbie Hancock's career transcended the evolution of jazz genres ranging from post-bop, modal, jazz funk, and fusion. He was the type of musician who could adopt a genre and make it his own. He was the pianist in one of the best rhythm sections in jazz history – the stellar 1960s Miles Davis Quintet. Hancock later went on to make several records under the Blue Note label during the 1960s, as well. Once the 1970s arrived, Hancock delved head first into the various jazz funk and fusion idioms, with his replacement of acoustic instruments, with electronic instruments. Some may not agree with Hancock's musical forks in the road, yet his importance in modern jazz cannot ever be diminished or overstated.

Some Key Albums and Musical Selections

King Cobra 🎵

I Have a Dream 🎵
Firewater 🎵

Maiden Voyage 𝓂   **The Eye of the Hurricane** 𝓋𝓰
Dolphin Dance 𝓂

Speak Like a Child 𝓂

Herbie Mann

Artist(s) Information

Herbert Jay Solomon – Flute, Saxophone, Bass Clarinet

Musical Background

Herbie Mann was an early pioneer of fusion jazz and world music. Mann began his jazz career as a bop flutist with artists such as Phil Woods, occasionally playing bass clarinet, tenor saxophone and solo flute. Mann eagerly delved into the later fusion genre during the mid-1960s and started his own record label in the 1970s, Embryo Records. Mann's most noted album, a classic, is *At the Village Gate*, recorded on Atlantic Records.

Some Key Albums and Musical Selections

Comin' Home Baby 𝓜   Summertime 𝓜   It Ain't Necessarily So 𝓜

Horace Silver

Artist(s) Information

Horace Silver - Piano

Musical Background

As a cofounder of the Jazz Messengers, along with Art Blakey, Horace Silver will always be important in modern jazz history. In 1956 Silver left the Jazz Messengers and blazed his own unique musical path which was reflected in his numerous recording under the Blue Note label. In the process Silver transitioned from bop to hard bop. He maintained a laudatory presence in the jazz scene for his entire lifetime and many of his albums are collector's items for jazz purists and club hoppers, alike.

Some Key Albums and Musical Selections

Jungle Juice E

The African Queen VG
Pretty Eyes E

Modern Jazz Classics

Too Much Sake 𝓋𝓰   **Sayonara Blues** ℰ   **Tokyo Blues** ℰ

Silver's Serenade ℰ
The Dragon Lady ℰ

Horace Tapscott

Artist(s) Information

Horace Elva Tapscott – Piano, Trombone

Musical Background

The founder of the Pan Afrikan Peoples Arkestra, formed in 1961, Horace Tapscott always displayed a transcendent outlook for his life and music. He played with like-minded artists such as Stanley Couch, Butch Morris, Jimmy Woods, and David Murray. "Otherworldly" aptly describes many of his notable recordings, yet *Aiee! The Phantom*, recorded on the Arabesque label remains a major standout.

Some Key Albums and Musical Selections

To the Great House *VG*
Aiee! The Phantom *M*
Mothership *VG*

The Goat and Ram Jam *E*
Inspiration of Silence *VG*

J.J. Johnson

Artist(s) Information

James Louis Johnson - Trombone

Musical Background

One of the few trombonists to have prominence in the bop jazz world. He started playing swing music, in which the trombone held a lot of prominence. Johnson seamlessly made the transition during the epoch of the bebop scene. He performed with many of the greats of the time including Charlie Parker. Johnson delved into pretty much all the modern jazz genres and even went Hollywood, as a film composer. Despite the multiplicity, Johnson always stayed true to the art form and created jazz standards along the way.

Some Key Albums and Musical Selections

Azure-Te E
Concepts in Blue VG

Minor Mist E
Fatback VG
Turnpike E

Neo 𝓔
Blues Waltz 𝓥𝓖
Minor Blues 𝓔
Lullaby of Jazzland 𝓔

A Must have for early Bop enthusiasts. Clifford Brown steals the show. 𝓔

Jackie McLean

Artist(s) Information

John Lenwood McLean – Alto Saxophone

Musical Background

Jackie McLean learned his craft as an adherent of Charlie Parker's bop school. He recorded with many of the greats including Gene Ammons, Charles Mingus, and Miles Davis. While staying true to his bop and hard bop roots, McLean ventured into the avant-garde. Many of his expressions were recorded under the Blue Note label in the 1960s. McClean held the torch and carried and preserved the tradition into the new millennium.

Some Key Albums and Musical Selections

On the Nile *M*   Soft Blue *E*
Climax *E*   Blue Fable *VG*

Jazz Crusaders

Artist(s) Information

Joe Sample – Piano
Stix Hooper – Drums
Wilton Felder - Saxophone
Wayne Henderson – Trombone
Robert "Pops" Popwell – Guitar

Musical Background

The Jazz Crusaders blazed a trail with their high-energy brand of hard bop in the 1960s. Their style enjoyed a strong following but their peak in popularity came after the group went crossover in 1971 and changed their name to "The Crusaders." By then the group went electric and maintained some of their early hard bop sentiments, yet it was drastically different. Great arguments over the two incarnations of the group still boil over today, however, the virtuoso expressions of the original Jazz Crusaders nests the group firmly in modern jazz history.

Some Key Albums and Musical Selections

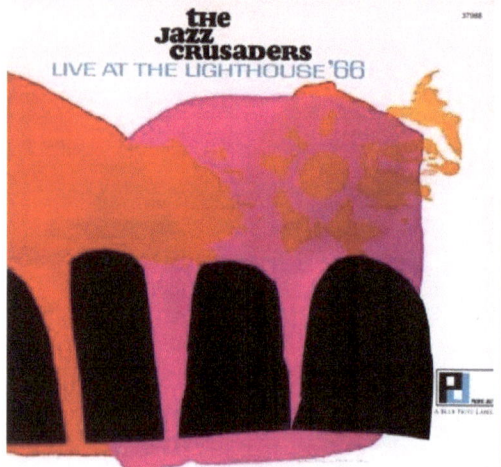
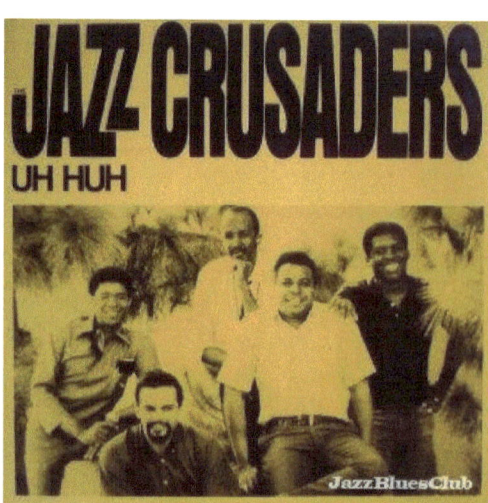

Miss It *VG*
Scratch *VG*

Blue Monday *M*
Air Waves *VG*
Night Theme *M*

Modern Jazz Classics

Eleanor Rigby 𝓜   The Emperor 𝓜   Impressions 𝓜

Freedom Sound ℰ
Outback ℰ
Bachafillen 𝓜
Firewater ℰ

Joe Henderson

Artist(s) Information

Joe Henderson – Tenor Saxophone

Musical Background

In a musical career that spanned over 40 years Joe Henderson started at a young age in the Detroit jazz scene in the mid-1950s. He played with the Horace Silver group for a time and provided a key solo in *Song for My Father*. Henderson played on 28 Blue Note recordings from 1963 to 68, being the leader on five of the albums. Even after the supposed "death" of modern jazz, Henderson held sway and released a seminal album, that helped usher in the post-bop rebirth of the 1980s, *State of the Tenor*, in 1986 that was recorded at the famed Village Vanguard in New York City.

Some Key Albums and Musical Selections

Punjab *E*
Short Story *vg*

Serenity *vg*
Brown's Town *vg*

Modern Jazz Classics

A Shade of Jade 𝓔   Mode for Joe 𝓜

Pedro's Time 𝓋𝑔
Escapade 𝓔

Inner Urge 𝓔 **El Barrio** 𝓜

Fire 𝓔

Joe Sample

Artist(s) Information

Joeseph Leslie Sample – Piano, Keyboards

Musical Background

A founding member of the famed Jazz Crusaders, Joe Sample's relevance in the jazz scene never let up. Even when the group morphed into the Crusaders, his playing style still held true to bop and hard bop sentiments. Sample proved that a true jazz musician could venture out commercially, gain adherents whom never were into straight ahead jazz, yet still retain that thing called "jazz."

Some Key Albums and Musical Selections

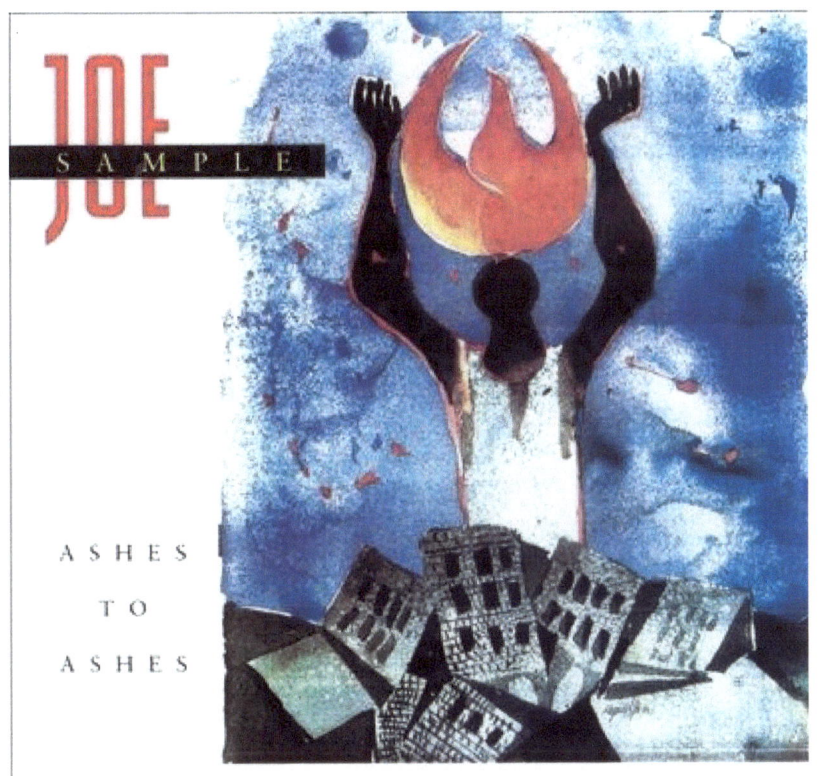

Ashes to Ashes 𝑉𝐺   Phoenix 𝑉𝐺

John Coltrane

Artist(s) Information

John William Coltrane – Tenor, Soprano, and Alto Saxophone

Musical Background

One of the most remarkable tales in the annals of jazz invokes the story of John Coltrane. He started his musical career as a youth playing in R & B bands. He entered the jazz scene and gained a very respectable reputation as a sideman, and eventually as a leader. He initially recorded on labels such as Prestige and Blue Note without the greatest fanfare. However, "Trane" went through some sort of "spiritual awakening" towards the end of the 1950s and blossomed into one of the most formidable players in all of modern jazz. The starting benchmark no doubt was the album *Giant Steps* recorded on the Atlantic label.

The rest, as they say, is "history." Coltrane never looked back after that point making some of the most awe inspiring recordings ever made in jazz history. It's mind boggling to contemplate that his amazing discography of work was recorded in only a 12 year period until he left this earth much too early at the age of 40.

Some Key Albums and Musical Selections

Impressions 𝓂

Modern Jazz Classics

Giant Steps 𝓔
Cousin Mary 𝓔
Spiral 𝓔

Syeeda's Song Flute 𝓔
Naima 𝓔
Mr. P.C. 𝓔

My Favorite Things 𝓜
Summertime 𝓔

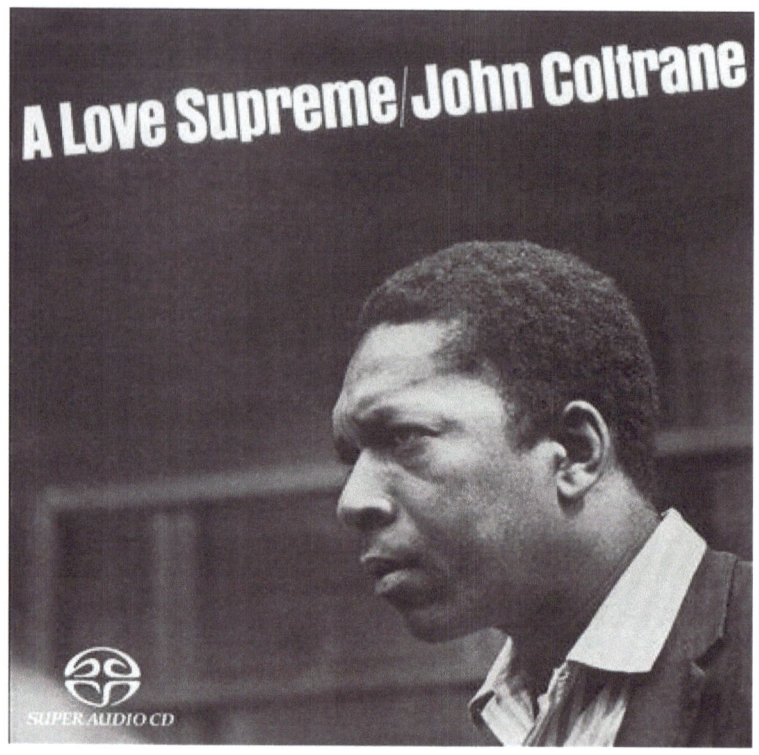

Acknowledgement 𝓂   Resolution 𝓂
Pursuance 𝓂   Psalm 𝓂

Crescent 𝓋𝑔
Wise One 𝓔
Lonnie's Lament 𝓔

Modern Jazz Classics

Africa *m* **Greensleeves** *E* **Blues Minor** *vg*
Song of the Underground Railroad *E*

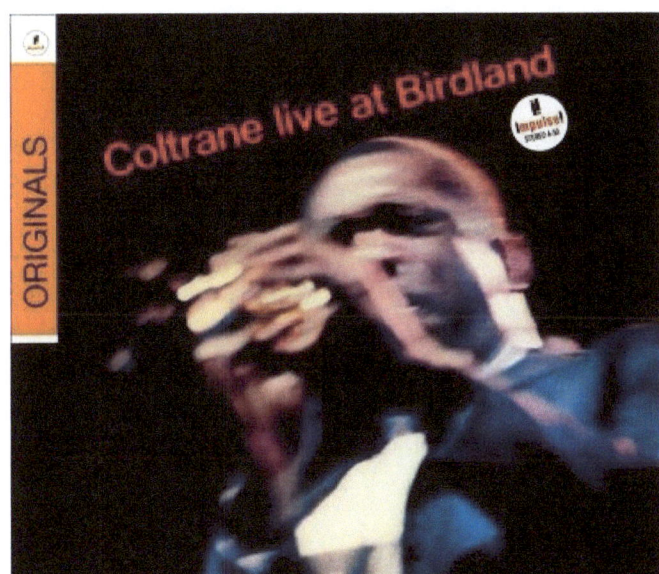

Afro Blue *E*
The Promise *E*
Alabama *m*

John Klemmer

Artist(s) Information

John Klemmer – Saxophones, Soprano Flute, Clarinet, Piano, Kalimba, Vocals

Musical Background

John Klemmer had the best of both worlds musically - theory and application. He studied saxophone and jazz improvisation with noted Chicago saxophonist and teacher Joe Daley. He attended the prestigious Interlochen's National Music Camp. He dabbled in every conceivable jazz style and played and/or produced musical idioms as varied as rock, pop, R & B, and adult contemporary. Klemmer's musical discography proves that maybe a person can do it all!

Some Key Albums and Musical Selections

Touch

Julian Joseph

Artist(s) Information

Julian Raphael Nathaniel Joseph - Piano

Musical Background

Born in London, England, Julian Joseph's talent splashed a wave throughout the post-bop jazz world. Joseph was one of the key young players to usher in the rebirth of modern jazz, especially the post-bop genre, along with players like Wynton Marsalis and others. His virtuosity on the piano set him apart from many of his contemporaries. He is not widely recorded but *The Language of Truth* is a standout and deserves its place in the lexicon.

Some Key Albums and Musical Selections

The Language of Truth *VG*   The Wash House *VG*

Kenny Garrett

Artist(s) Information

Kenny Garrett – Alto and Soprano Saxophone, Flute

Musical Background

As a youngster Kenny Garrett played in the Duke Ellington Orchestra and in Miles Davis' fusion band. A few years later he played in the Mel Lewis Orchestra, playing the music of Thad Jones, and also the Dannie Richmond Quartet, focusing on Charles Mingus' music. He first recorded as a leader in 1984 with the album *Introducing Kenny Garrett*. His finely crafted musical expressions always displayed a reverence for greats of the past. This should be no surprise considering he was blessed to play along with such greats as Art Blakey, Pharoah Sanders, Herbie Hancock, Bobby Hutcherson, Elvin Jones, along with a host of other jazz greats.

Some Key Albums and Musical Selections

Oriental Towaway Zone

Modern Jazz Classics

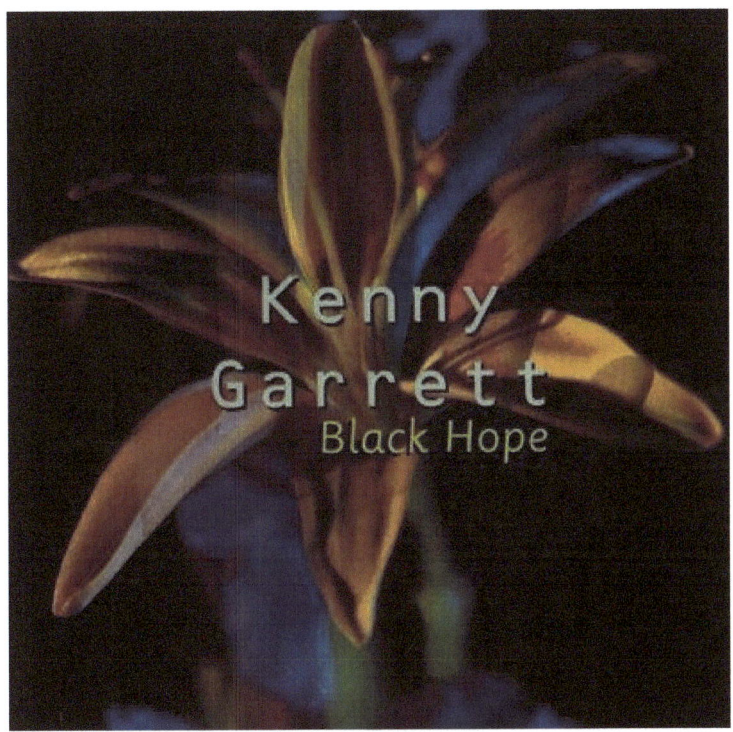

Tacit Dance **Spanish-Go-Round**

The entire album does a respectable homage to Coltrane.

Lee Morgan

Artist(s) Information

Edward Lee Morgan – Trumpet, Flugelhorn

Musical Background

One of the most agile trumpeters ever in jazz history, Lee Morgan blazed a path through the modern jazz era that was rivaled but never surpassed. He played an important role as a trumpeter for Art Blakey's Jazz Messengers in the late 1950s. Ultimately he became a sideman and leader on numerous albums recorded on the Blue Note label – many of them became jazz classics. The tune *Sidewinder*, recorded in 1963, was Morgan's greatest commercial success, but did little to reveal his true musical genius. He would later cautiously release a string of classic albums on Blue Note during the 1960s. His life was tragically cut short when he was shot on stage at New York's Slug's Saloon by a long-time girlfriend. Tragic is an understatement for many who proclaim Morgan as the greatest virtuoso trumpeter in the modern jazz age.

Some Key Albums and Musical Selections

Even early on, Lee Morgan had the chops! Nuff Said.

Modern Jazz Classics

Yes I Can, No You Can't 🆅🅶   Trapped 🅴
The Gigolo 🅼   You Go To My Head 🅼

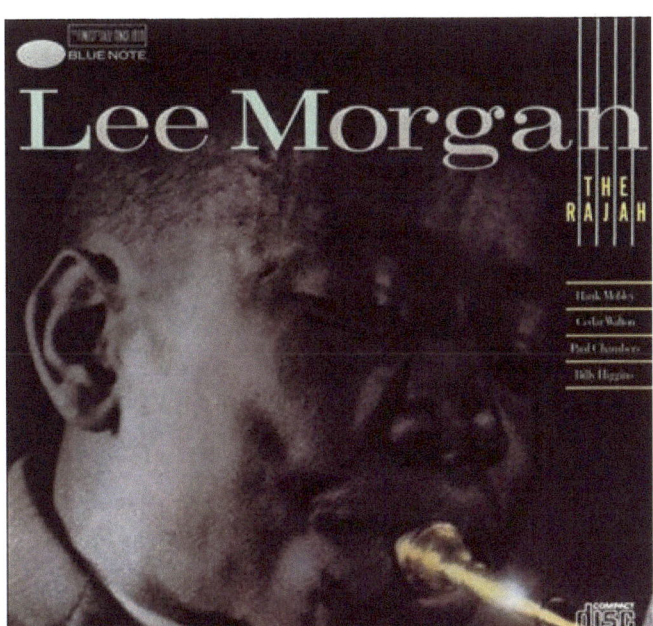

The Rajah 🅴
Davisamba 🅴
Once in My Lifetime 🅴

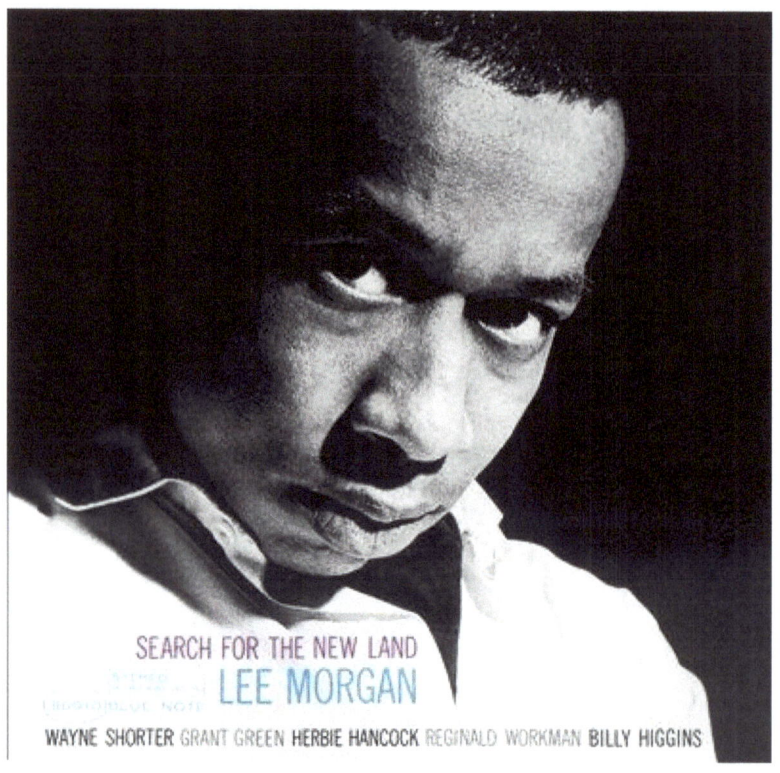

Search for the New Land 𝓂   Mr. Kenyatta ℰ   Melancholee ℰ

Afreaka 𝓋𝑔
Mickey's Tune ℰ

Modern Jazz Classics

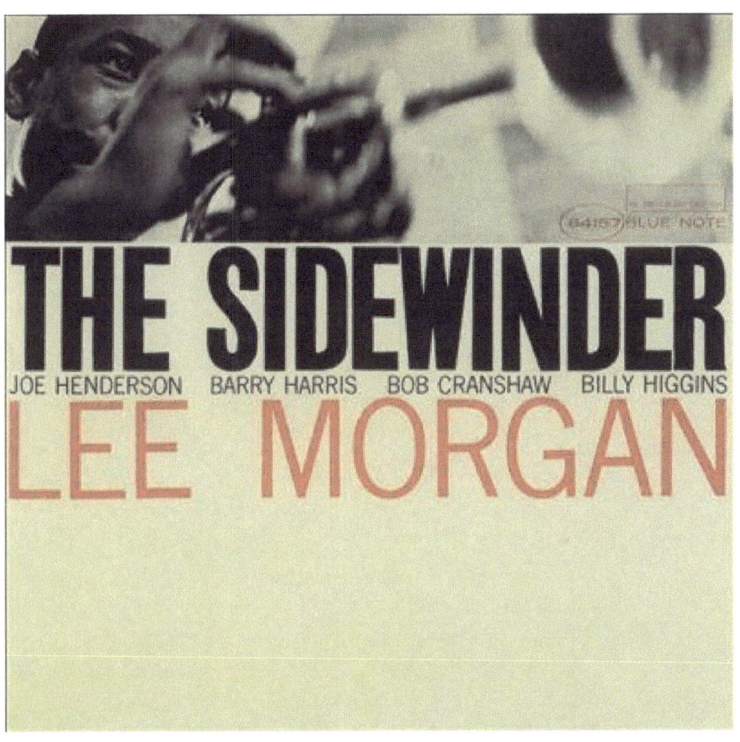

Totem Pole *vg*   Gary's Notebook *E*

Avotcha One *vg*

Tom Cat *vg*   Exotique *E*

Desert Moonlight *vg*
Edda *vg*
Venus Di Mildew *vg*

McCoy Tyner

Artist(s) Information

Alfred McCoy Tyner - Piano

Musical Background

McCoy Tyner's musical career started to blossom as a sideman for Benny Golson in 1960, but it went into full orbit when Tyner became a sideman for John Coltrane's incomparable group from 1960 to 1965. Tyner displayed a percussive piano style that could only be matched by past stride piano greats such as Fat's Waller or Art Tatum. Tyner proved to be a force of his own as a leader and continued to speak his own unique dialect of modern jazz.

Some Key Albums and Musical Selections

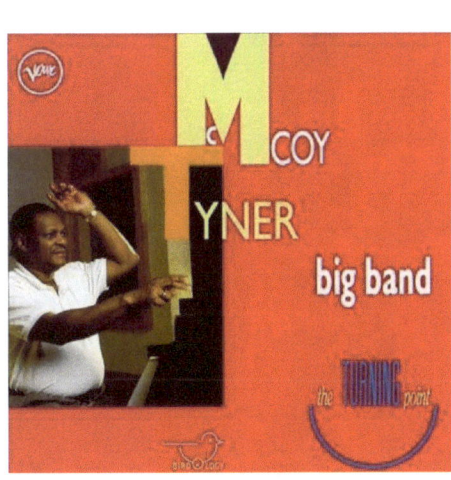 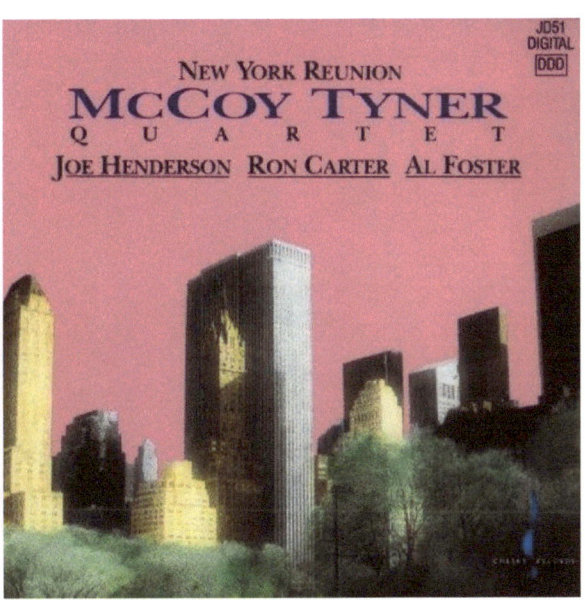

Angel Eyes   **Home**

Contemplation

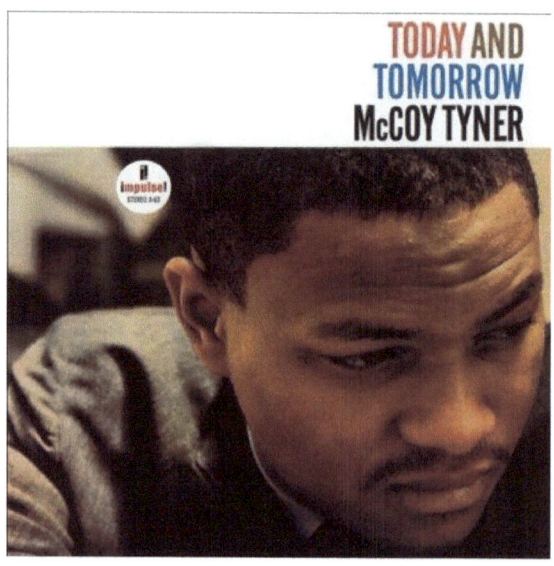

Contemporary Focus

Miles Davis

Artist(s) Information

Miles Dewey Davis III

Musical Background

As it relates to the modern jazz era few, if any, ever could embody the entire history like Miles Davis. Davis grew up during the formation of the bop era and played with its very key figures like Charlie Parker and Dizzy Gillespie. However, Davis did not possess the virtuosity of either. Such would serve to not be any impedance at all – Davis simply went his own way and became one of the key figures in the development of "cool" or "West coast" jazz. His discography plainly shows a musician who was not scared to change his style or to move to new forms of expression. Bop, cool, modal, fusion, and advant-garde are all present in various albums led by Davis. Regardless of style, Davis became a master at playing less notes to evoke more feeling. No one did that quite like Miles.

Some Key Albums and Musical Selections

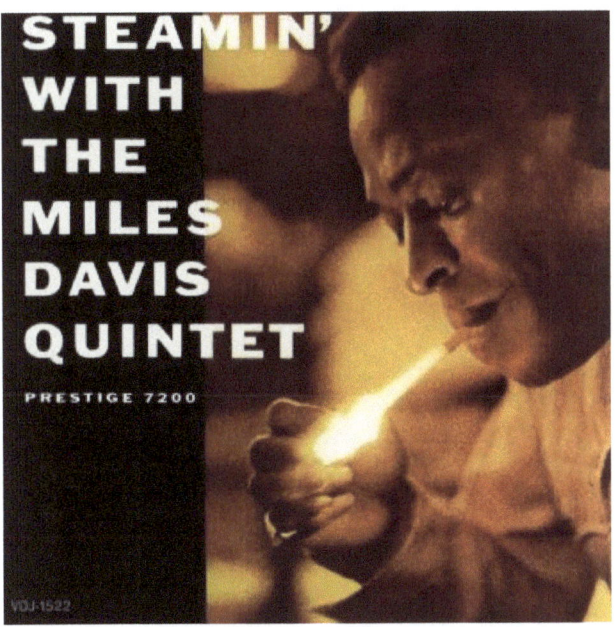

Surrey with the Fringe on Top *vg*   Diane *vg*
Well You Needn't *vg*

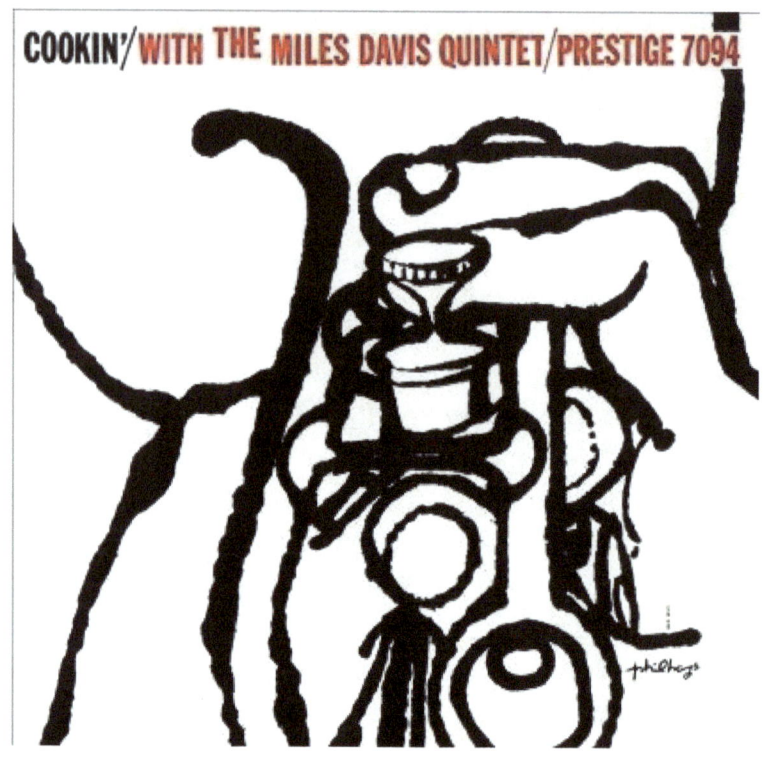

Blues by Five 𝒱𝒢   **Airegin** ℰ

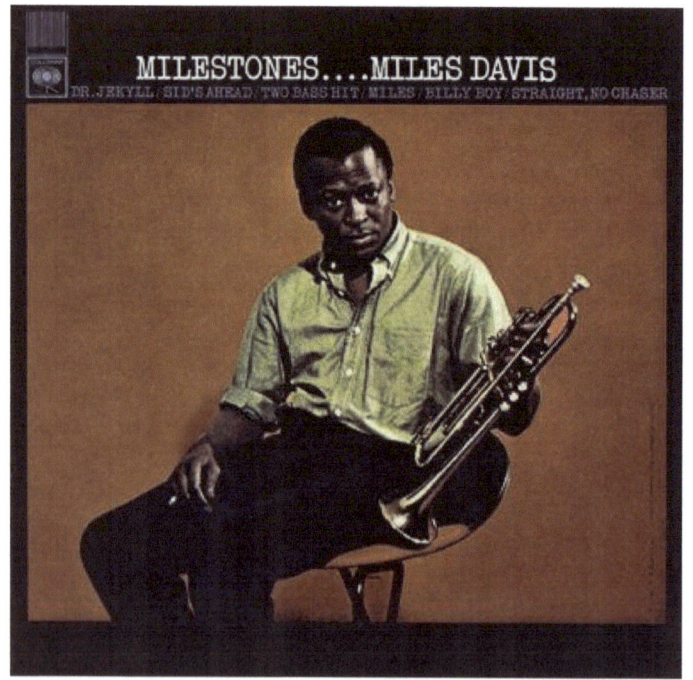

Miles ℰ

Modern Jazz Classics

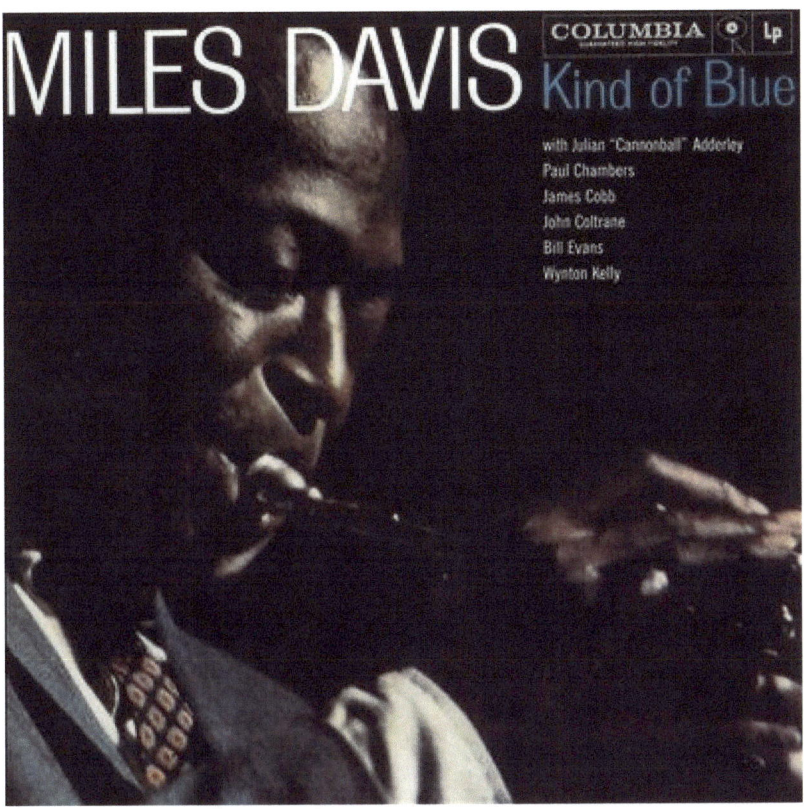

So What 𝓂   All Blues 𝓂   Flamenco Sketches 𝓔

Teo 𝓂

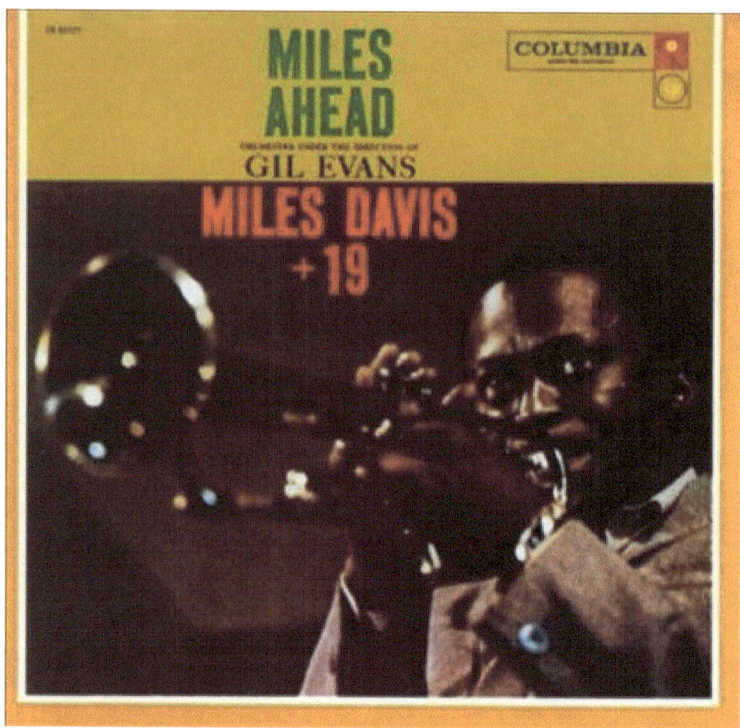

Miles Ahead 𝄞   New Rhumba 𝄞

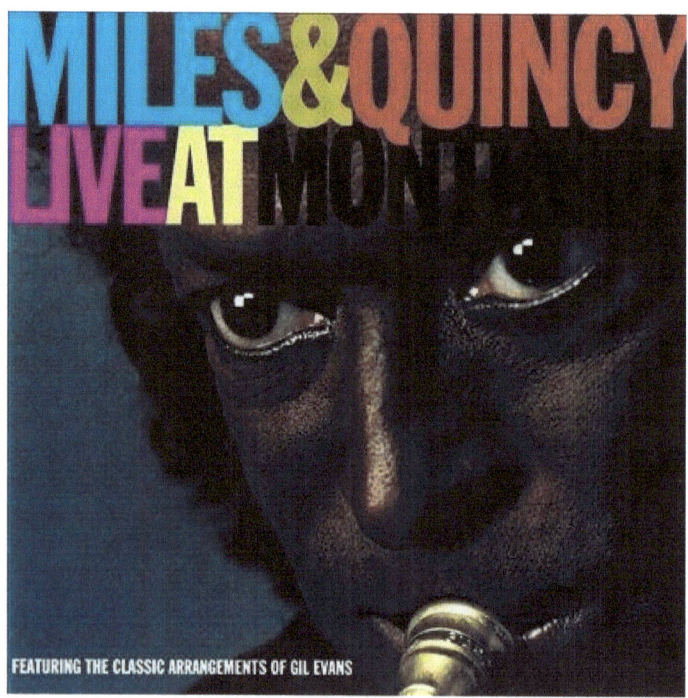

Solea 𝄞

Milt Jackson

Artist(s) Information

Milton Jackson – Vibraphone, Piano

Musical Background

One of the key vibraphonists in the bop era, Milt Jackson remained relevant through every incantation of expression during the modern jazz movement. Indefatigable as a recording artist with multiple dozens of recordings as a leader and sideman with a litany of recording labels. All in all, Jackson is a true modern jazz icon that must be heard to be truly understood.

Some Key Albums and Musical Selections

A Time and a Place 🎵   We Dwell in Our Hearts 🎵

Early Bop Vibe at its best.

That's the Way It Is

Nancy Wilson

Artist(s) Information

Nancy Wilson – Jazz Vocals

Musical Background

If there were a vocalist that could be described as great at every genre of music, Nancy Wilson would be at the top of the list. Wilson could sing the blues, R & B, pop tunes, jazz, and everything in between. Her over 70 albums and multitudinous awards, like her three Grammys, bear witness to her timeless talent. Her album *Nancy Wilson/Cannonball Adderley* is viewed by many jazz adherents as the finest jazz vocal album of the modern jazz era.

Some Key Albums and Musical Selections

Never Will I Marry 𝓜   Old Country 𝓜   Happy Talk ℰ
The Masquerade is Over 𝓜   Little Unhappy Boy 𝓜   Teaneck ℰ

Nina Simone

Artist(s) Information

Eunice Kathleen Waymon – Jazz Vocals, Piano

Musical Background

Nina Simone was a force to be reckoned with her often fiery brand of jazz vocalism. She stood up for civil rights during her life in a way that most men would have shuttered. She recorded more than 40 albums and was always socially conscious. She blew the roof off the music world with her rendition of the song *Mississippi Goddam*, which was her response to the June 12, 1963, murder of Medgar Evers and the September 15, 1963, bombing of the 16th Street Baptist Church in Birmingham, Alabama, that killed four young black girls and partially blinded a fifth girl. Musically important for sure – yet even more important historically, Nina Simone's inner strength and beauty has to be heard musically for regular people to even come close to understanding.

Some Key Albums and Musical Selections

I Loves You Porgy *E*
Mississippi Goddam *E*
Sinnerman *M*
See Line Woman *E*
Break Down and Let It All Out *E*
Four Women *E*
Wild Is the Wind *M*
Don't Let Me Be Misunderstood *M*

Oliver Nelson

Artist(s) Information

Oliver Nelson – Alto, Soprano, and Tenor Saxophone

Musical Background

Just as well known, if not more so, for being a composer and arranger as player, Oliver Nelson proved to be an invaluable resource as he worked as an arranger on large ensemble albums for Cannonball Adderley, Sonny Rollins, Eddie "Lockjaw" Davis, Johnny Hodges, Wes Montgomery, Buddy Rich, Jimmy Smith, and Gene Ammons. Nelson also worked on television projects that included *Ironside*, *Night Gallery*, *Columbo*, *The Six Million Dollar Man,* and *Longstreet*. Films scored by Nelson include *Death of a Gunfighter* (1969), *Skullduggery* (1970) and *Zig Zag* (1970). Nelson was greatly involved in jazz education and published a book of jazz practice exercises, *Patterns for Improvisation,* that was published in 1966 that remains highly regarded to this day.

Some Key Albums and Musical Selections

Stolen Moments

Ornette Coleman

Artist(s) Information

Randolph Denard Ornette Coleman – Alto and Tenor Saxophone, Violin, Trumpet

Musical Background

If the intention was to turn the jazz world on its head and create a firestorm, Ornette Coleman succeeded. Coleman certainly was one of the lonely major initiators of the free jazz movement in the late 1950s. Enduring all the slings and arrows of the critics of the time, Coleman eventually formed his legendary group that initially included Don Cherry (Cornet), Charlie Haden (Bass), and Billy Higgins (Drums). Coleman eventually recorded several albums on the Atlantic label, which has influenced modern jazz ever since.

Some Key Albums and Musical Selections

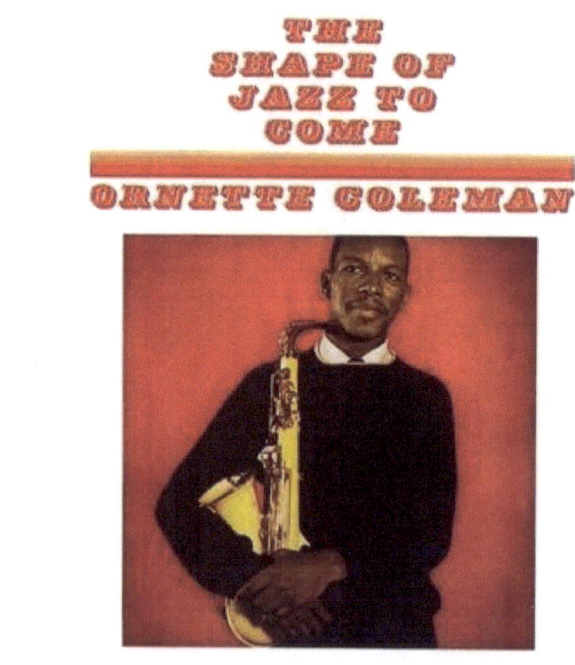

Lonely Woman 🎵   Eventually 🎵   Peace 🎵
Congeniality 🎵   Chronology 🎵

Pharoah Sanders

Artist(s) Information

Farrell Sanders - Saxophone

Musical Background

Pharoah Sanders played with John Coltrane's group in the mid-1960s. Sanders displayed a forceful "sheets of sound" style exemplified by Coltrane. After contributing to some advant-garde classics under Coltrane's leadership, Sanders ventured out and made several thrilling recordings under his own leadership on the Impulse! label. Sanders' music endures and continues to be completely thrilling and relevant today.

Some Key Albums and Musical Selections

You've Got to Have Freedom 𝓂

Upper Egypt and Lower Egypt 𝓂

Hum-Allah-Hum-Allah... 𝓂

Rahsaan Roland Kirk

Artist(s) Information

Ronald Theodore Kirk – Tenor Saxophone, Clarinet, Flute. Keyboard, Percussion

Musical Background

Well-heeled in all aspects of jazz theory, Roland Kirk masterfully blazed his own musical trail. He was a multi-instrumentalist – literary playing two or more wind instruments at once. His music reflected his social consciousness and interest in Black history. He became a master at circular breathing and could sustain notes for extended periods of time. To call many of his socially relevant and musically exciting works innovative would be quite an understatement.

Some Key Albums and Musical Selections

 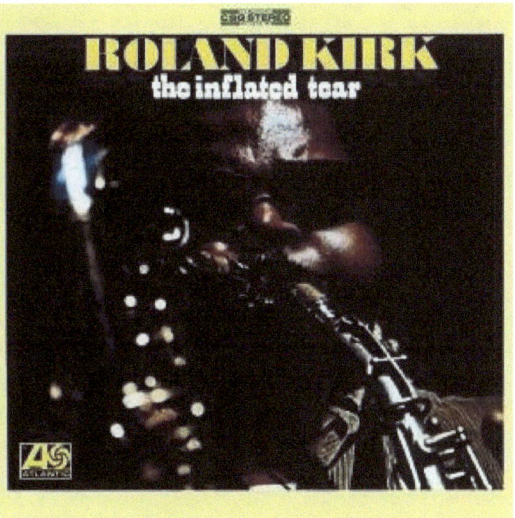

Never Can Say Goodbye 𝓔

A Handful of Fives 𝓥𝓰
Fly By Night 𝓔
Lovelleveliloqui 𝓔

Ramsey Lewis

Artist(s) Information

Ramsey Emmanuel Lewis Jr. – Piano, Keyboards

Musical Background

Ramsey Lewis was one of the few jazz pianists of the modern jazz era who succeeded at attracting a wide audience beyond jazz circles. He adroitly fused bluesy soul and funk with his jazz style and it went over well with both jazz adherents and neophytes alike. By 1966, Lewis was one of the nation's most successful jazz pianists, topping the charts with *The In Crowd*, *Hang On Sloopy*, and *Wade in the Water*. His renown and cachet in jazz circles continued on in later decades while Lewis entertained and taught the gospel of jazz to students in schools and over the radio waves.

Some Key Albums and Musical Selections

The "In" Crowd *VG*   Love Theme from Spartacus *E*

Roy Hargrove

Artist(s) Information

Roy Anthony Hargrove – Trumpet, Fluegelhorn

Musical Background

One of the major young figures of the 1980s post-bop renaissance. Unlike Wynton Marsalis and other young players, Hargrove unhesitantly indulged in funk, soul, along with other variations. A fan favorite because of his accessibility to both jazzphiles and neophytes. The Grammy award winning Hargrove always paid homage to the elders and took the opportunity to record with some of the major jazz musicians on *With the Tenors of Our Time*, including Joe Henderson, Stanley Turrentine, and Johnny Griffin. Hargrove's music aptly proves that you can move forward and still stay true to the past simultaneously.

Some Key Albums and Musical Selections

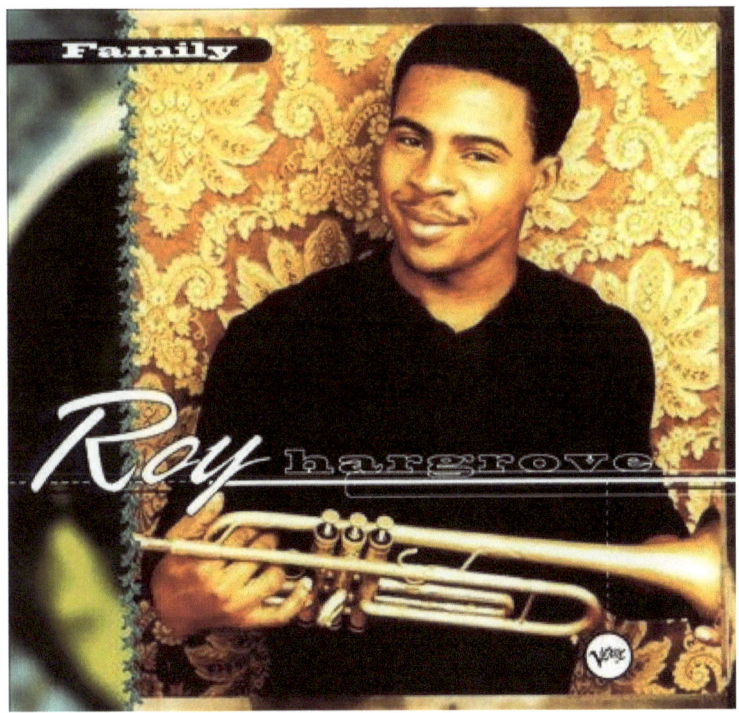

The Thirteenth Floor

Sonny Rollins

Artist(s) Information

Walter Theodore Rollins – Tenor and Soprano Saxophone

Musical Background

The epitome of the 1950s bop saxophonist, Sonny Rollins blazed a path that certainly influenced other musicians of the time. Rollin's recorded musical output was always ever more progressive and there was never any real hint of routine banality. Many of his compositions have become jazz standards. Throughout his career Rollins never ceased in his journey for musical nirvana.

Some Key Albums and Musical Selections

St. Thomas *VG*
Strode Rode *VG*

Alfie's Theme *VG*
He's Younger Than You Are *VG*
Street Runner With Child *E*
Transition Team for Minor *E*
On Impulse! *VG*

Thad Jones

Artist(s) Information

Thaddeus Joseph Jones – Trumpet, Cornet, Flugelhorn

Musical Background

Steeped in the bop world, Thad Jones capably performed in the modern jazz era along with his brothers Hank and Elvin Jones. He was one of the few musicians who could competently play with the paradoxical Thelonious Monk. He played the cornet on Monk's *5 by Monk by 5* album. Jones traveled the world, lived out his days in Europe, and his playing reflected his appreciation for life beyond the social, physical, and mental boundaries of the U.S.

Some Key Albums and Musical Selections

April in Paris

Thelonious Monk

Artist(s) Information

Thelonious Sphere Monk - Piano

Musical Background

One of the most logically expressive pianists in modern jazz, yet one of the most challenging to play with for even the most experienced musician. Actually Monk was a crucial person in the development of bebop, just like Charlies Parker and Dizzy Gillespie. What set Mink apart was his very unorthodox use of time and spacing of his musical notes. This along with his quixotic personality likely prevented him from gaining his just due sooner in life. However, after Monk released *Brilliant Corners* on the Original Jazz Classics label, his greatness could never be shoved to the side again. Monk's rightful place is among the greatest jazz musicians and composers of the modern jazz age.

Some Key Albums and Musical Selections

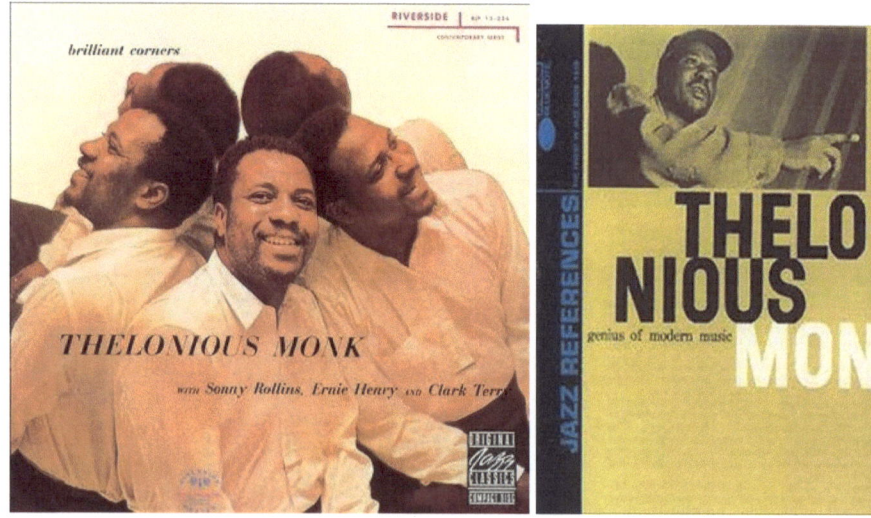

Brilliant Corners *vg*
Pannonica *vg*

The Album is truly a Must Have.
Full of Bop Classics! *m*

Tina Brooks

Artist(s) Information

Harold Floyd Brooks – Tenor Saxophone

Musical Background

Brooks' first professional work came in 1951 with rhythm and blues pianist Sonny Thompson, and, in 1955, Brooks played with vibraphonist Lionel Hampton. In the late 1950s through the early 1960s Brooks recorded some very notable albums under the Blue Note label. His lyrical style and beautiful tone is put on wonderful display on those albums. He unfortunately only recorded four albums and died early in life at the age of 42. Despite the tragic circumstances, Brooks left the world a wonderful musical legacy.

Some Key Albums and Musical Selections

Good Old Soul 𝄋 Theme for Doris 𝄋 True Blue 𝄋

Wayne Shorter

Artist(s) Information

Wayne Shorter – Tenor and Soprano Saxophone

Musical Background

As one of the members of Mile Davis' famed quintet of the 1960s, Wayne Shorter could have rested on those laurels. Incredibly, Shorter proceeded to record some of the most masterful albums ever in modern jazz history on the Blue Note label during his time with the Miles Davis Quintet. He switch gears from the modal jazz he was playing to a fusion style in the 1970s. His group, Weather Report, a disappointment to some jazz purists, was a commercial success. No worries because no matter what could be said about the fusion pieces, Shorter's "straight ahead" recordings are shining moments in modern jazz history.

Some Key Albums and Musical Selections

Tom Thumb 𝑣𝑔

Witch Hunt ℰ
Speak No Evil 𝑚

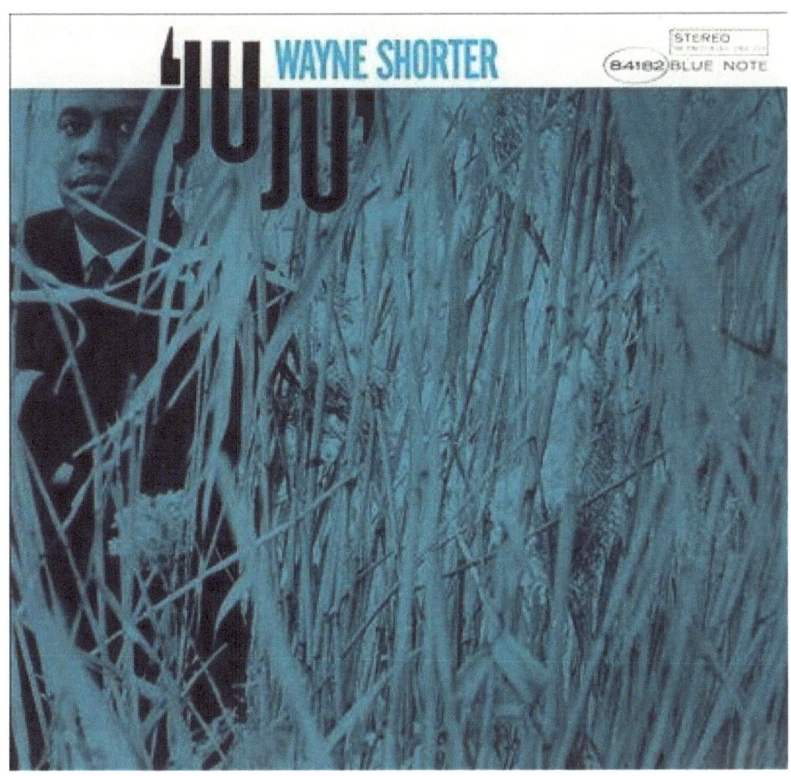

Juju *vg*	Deluge *e*
House of Jade *e*	Majong *m*
Yes or No *vg*	Twelve More Bars to Go *vg*

Night Dreamer *vg*
Oriental Folk Song *e*
Charcoal Blues *e*
Armagedon *m*

502 Blues (Drinkin' and Drivin') *E*
Footprints *E*

El Gaucho *E*
Chief Crazy Horse *E*

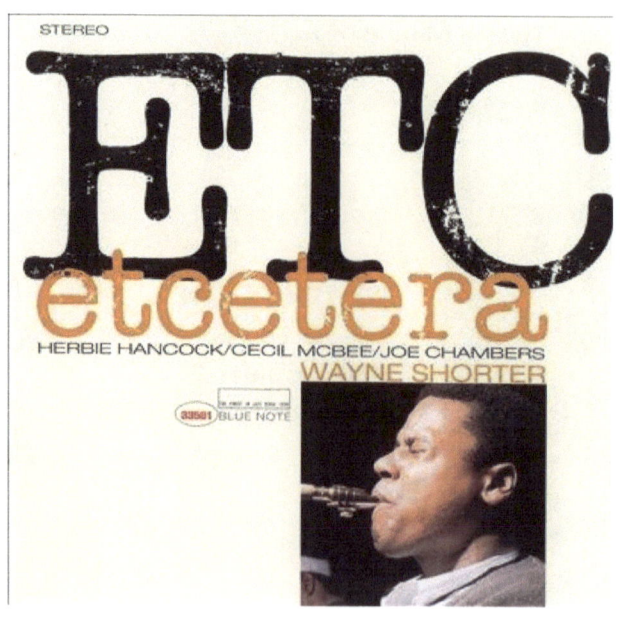

Penelope *VG*
Barracudas (General Assembly) *M*
Indian Song *E*

Wynton Kelly

Artist(s) Information

Wynton Charles Kelly - Piano

Musical Background

Despite tragically dying at the age of 39, Wynton Kelly left the world with some very import contributions to modern jazz. Kelly attracted the most attention as part of Miles Davis' band from 1959, including an appearance on the trumpeter's *Kind of Blue*, often mentioned as the best-selling jazz album ever. Kelly recorded his best work while working with Paul Chambers (Bass) and Jimmy Cobb (Drums) as sidemen, along with others such as Kenny Burrell (Guitar) and Candido Camero (Conga). Paul chambers died in 1969 and Kelly departed soon after in 1971, yet not before leaving their mark in modern jazz history.

Some Key Albums and Musical Selections

It's All Right *E*
South Seas *M*
Kelly Roll *VG*
Escapade *VG*

Wynton Marsalis

Artist(s) Information

Wynton Leason Marsalis - Trumpet

Musical Background

Raised in a very musical family and graduating from under Art Blakey's tutelage as a side man in the Jazz Messengers, Wynton Marsalis is probably the most visible of the young players who ushered in the post-bop movement on the 1980s. Marsalis proved to be an adept player and grew into greater prominence as a jazz scholar. His awards and recognition were plentiful including serving as artistic director for Jazz at Lincoln Center, nine Grammy Awards, several honorary degrees, along with a host of other awards. At times he had been accused of being a jazz "doctrinaire," yet his profound contributions to the preservation of modern jazz cannot be understated.

Some Key Albums and Musical Selections

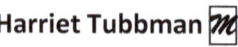

Harriet Tubbman

Yusef Lateef

Artist(s) Information

William Emanuel Huddleston – Tenor Saxophone, Flute, Oboe, Bassoon, Bamboo Flute, Shehnai, Arghul, Koto, Piano, Vocals

Musical Background

Smooth and airy are accurate descriptions of Yusef Lateef's sound. His multi-instrumentation abilities proved to be beneficial in the development of his unique sound. Lateef began recording as a leader in 1957 for Savoy records. His sound as reflected by his 1961 albums *Into Something* and *Eastern Sound* is said to have been a major influence on other musicians of the time.

Some Key Albums and Musical Selections

Love Theme from Spartacus 𝓜
Love Theme from the Robe 𝓔

About the Author

At the helm of Uptown Media Joint Ventures, K Kelly is following his passion of helping authors get their viable stories published and marketed to their readers! This passion includes expanding the audiences for recording artists and freelance journalists, as well!

K Kelly is an avid Modern Jazz enthusiast. He proudly owns a vintage collection of over 1000 classic jazz CDs. His first jazz book, a buying guide, *Best of the Best Modern Jazz* was an effort to compile his significant knowledge of the genre to assist others who want to develop and enjoy their own modern jazz collection. *Modern jazz Classics* expands on the concept by adding biographical information for key musicians of the modern jazz era.

K Kelly is a contributor to Robert Fleming's noted work *Free Jazz* and *Rasta, Babylon, Burning*, a comprehensive book on the music and culture of reggae.

Modern Jazz Classics

Full Color Edition

K Kelly McElroy

www.ingramcontent.com/pod-product-compliance
Lightning Source LLC
Chambersburg PA
CBHW041958150426
43194CB00002B/55